THE HERO AND THE DRAGON:

BUILDING CHRISTIAN CHARACTER THROUGH FANTASY FICTION

Published by Booklocker.com, Inc., Port Charlotte, Florida.

Printed in the United States of America on acid-free paper.

Booklocker.com, Inc.
2012

First Edition

THE HERO AND THE DRAGON:

BUILDING CHRISTIAN CHARACTER THROUGH FANTASY FICTION

Andrew Boll

Dedication:

To my parents,
who first put the Sword into my hands
and showed me how to wield it…

…and to my wife,
who often shines the Light upon my path
when I would wander into darkness.

Table of Contents

Introduction: The Journey Begins...

As a high school English teacher, I often have parents ask for my advice concerning their children's reading habits. The fact that their children even HAVE reading habits gives me a great deal of encouragement right off the bat, and the fact that they care enough to be interested in *what* their kids are reading makes my heart run over. So if you are reading this book for yourself, you're making a great investment into your literary future (if I may say so myself). And if you are reading it for the sake of a child, you are of the most valuable class of hero that exists today.

Yes, fantasy fiction is all the rage these days. In a broad sense, fantasy deals with any story that deviates from the normal boundaries of reality; magic, mythical creatures, supernatural phenomenon, science fiction, and even some pseudo-historical fiction. While this book focuses mainly on "classical" fantasy (generally defined by swords, magic, and monsters), there may be many elements and themes that pertain to other corners of the world of fantasy literature. Especially note the first chapter on the "Hero's Journey", which serves as the motif for a great majority of ALL fiction, past and present.

There are dangers along the path of fantasy fiction, just as there are dangers along the path of life, but there is nothing that a properly trained and equipped warrior can't overcome. The forest can be dark and threatening at times, but for the most part it is beautiful and peaceful. There are monsters lurking in the shadows, but there is also untold treasure to be won. The important thing is to know beforehand what you are up against and how to properly defend yourself. So is this book an endorsement or a criticism of fantasy fiction? Well, a little bit of both.

Who is this guy and where did he come from?

I started exploring other worlds at a fairly young age. Thankfully, my parents encouraged reading, and early on I developed a love of literature that would eventually lead me to a career of teaching young people how to understand and appreciate stories. Countless hours of my own youth were spent next to the heat register behind the couch with a stack of books by my side. But that is only a vague recollection...

My true memories are ones of being whisked away on wild adventures into unknown lands inhabited by strange creatures and filled with peril. The living room, the bookshelf, the couch, the end table; all of them would disappear in a swirling vortex as I gladly tumbled down another literary wormhole into worlds born of imagination and mindcraft.

But none of it was real!... That's what some of you may be thinking right now; that it was all just a waste of time, a conspicuous squandering of precious fleeting youth and life that could have been spent frolicking in green meadows and climbing trees and bruising shins and making mud pies and all the other things that kids were really *meant* to do. Not to worry- I spent many an hour doing all of those things as well. I played *hard* growing up, and many times I could spend the entire day being outside without plastic guns, without sports balls, even sometimes without friends when they were not to be found. In today's age of manic distraction, not many kids are able to spend five minutes without "toys" of some sort before they start to drive their parents batty. But *because* of my reading adventures, I was never bored when left to my own devices.

You see, the same miracle happened when I stepped outside the back door into the world as when I opened a new book behind the couch. Before my very eyes, the grass melted and became a wind-tossed sea teeming with slimy serpents with bulging eyes and long tentacles. Just beneath them lie chests filled with gold and silver coins, gems and jewels, pearl-encrusted goblets, and all sorts of other fantastic treasures. The patio deck under my feet became the deck of a sturdy sailing ship, outfitted with cannons and masts and a huge wooden wheel for steering. The four corners of my yard became the four corners of the Earth itself, and beyond. I tell you, there wasn't a stick lying in that yard that did not become a sword or a spear or an arrow. There wasn't a bush or tree or shrub that didn't daily become a dragon or some other hideous beast waiting to do battle with any bold adventurer who dared trespass beyond the Woodpile and the mighty Retaining Wall.

Wasted!? Why, I squeezed more life out of each blessed day than many of my contemporaries could manage in a whole year! Who can say that they had a childhood to compare with mine? I was a veritable Gulliver or Odysseus by the age of nine, and the adventures *never* got old. On rainy days, or in the winter time, the miracle came into our home. The couch or bed became a desert island, a comforting home base from which I would gather supplies and set out to explore the basement dungeons or closet jungles. Or sometimes, it would simply be time to retreat to my heat register behind the couch and refuel my imagination for another day with a good book.

Undoubtedly, there are a few readers out there still smirking and saying to themselves, *Yes, but none of it was real.* In response to which I would like to present exhibit "A": myself. No biographical narrative, no history, no encyclopedia entry could have ever touched me in a way that those stories did. They were as real to me as anything in the world, because they became a *part* of me; they are *my* history. They shaped me into what I am today and gave me the character traits that have helped me to be a better Christian, a better husband, a better father, and an all-around better *man.*

> *"The gift of fantasy has meant more to me than my talent for absorbing positive knowledge."*
>
> ~Albert Einstein

So what's the point? Why this book?

Ah, I see you don't beat around the bush much, do you? Very well, on with it. As I continued to grow, I became more and more interested in stories dealing with things outside of the normal boundaries of this world: Fantasy. My third grade teacher, Mrs. Knight, introduced me to Madeleine L'Engle's world of fantasy/science fiction by reading us "A Wrinkle in Time". I was enthralled with the story, the world, the characters, the conflict between good and evil that spanned across time and space...and I couldn't help but feel that they all had some connection to *me*. Although I understood perfectly well that it was only fiction and could never really happen (I was imaginative, not delusional), I felt a connection between what was happening to the characters in the story and certain events in my own life. With this epiphany, there was a vague sense of familiarity that grew stronger and stronger, until eventually I was to realize that this "connection" was what had always drawn me toward stories of fantasy and adventure.

I continued trying to grasp this connection as I got older and read more stories, now reading them with *intention*. Characters in the stories were often searching for something, and now I was searching for something. *There* was a connection that tied me more closely to the genre. The thing was, I really *liked* the heroes of the stories that I read. They were so much like *me*, in some ways. And the differences were such that they made me *want* to be more like them.

By now, I was finding fantasy adventures stories in other sources besides just books. My favorite movie growing up was *Willow*, a movie about a dwarf-like creature who leaves home to help a lost baby and ends up trying to help save the world. That movie inspired me in so many ways, shaping me and reinforcing the kind of person I knew God wanted me to become.

When I was in the eighth grade, I acquired a Super Nintendo from a classmate. Among the dozen or so games that he sold to me along with the system was a little-known game called *Chrono Trigger*. It was a "role-playing" game, where you play out an adventure controlling one or more characters, making decisions for them and experiencing their "story." When I finally took the time to learn how to play it, it was a truly life-changing event. The adventure was of such quality that I shall always remember it. There were swords and magic and time travel, and above all it had a young man my age who was willing to sacrifice much for the sake of others. He is a part of me still today. The "connection" that I had always felt with these stories became much more real to

> *"Fantasies are more than substitutes for unpleasant realities; they are also dress rehearsals, plans. All acts performed in the world begin in the imagination."*
>
> *~Barbara Grizzuti Harrison*

me after that, and God began to open my eyes to the link between the heroes of fantasy and His warriors of faith.

Perils on the Forest Path

So far, this has been nothing but a promotion of fantasy fiction for young Christians. That isn't really the intention of this book. As you can see, my path was relatively free from brambles during my early years of exploring the fantasy genre. Thanks be to God that through His Spirit I was encountering this new world through the framework of my Christian faith. Thanks be to God for giving me strong Christian parents who nourished my faith (weak and flimsy as it has often been) through the Word of God, and who modeled for me what it meant for a Christian warrior to exhibit the heroic traits and ideals about which I was reading. These are distinct advantages that I had as I set off down the path of fantasy fiction, and these advantages enabled me to survive many of the dangers along the way. Not every young man or woman is fortunate to have the blessings of faith and family in their lives, and the forest can be dark indeed for these travelers.

I must admit that there are elements to fantasy fiction that can be a tremendous stumbling block to young Christians (or young non-Christians, for that matter). Our sinful nature and curiosity give a certain allure to power, magic, brute force, and forbidden knowledge. Not all stories of adventure properly warn readers of these dangers; indeed, many of them encourage these reckless pursuits. That is why it is vitally important for young readers (and their parents) to understand what these elements often mean and the real-life dangers that lie behind them. At the same time, it would be a tragic waste if, in an effort to avoid the snares and pitfalls, we were to throw out everything that is good in fantasy fiction, because there is a LOT of good.

I can't make the decision whether fantasy fiction is right for you or for your children. I can only provide guidance and advice concerning the paths that I have already explored. As with any genre, there is some amazingly good literature out there and some really terrible stuff. Hopefully this book will help you know which it is when you come across it.

Journey through the forest with boldness but caution. Learn from every encounter. Gain the strength and wisdom you will need ahead from the challenges you overcome. Help others along the way. Keep your weapons close, and keep them sharp. Know your enemies and their weaknesses. Know yourself and your own weaknesses. Flee whenever necessary, but fight bravely whenever possible. Savor every step, because the path can only be travelled once. And at the

> *"I think one of the best guides to telling you who you are – and I think children use it all the time for this purpose – is fantasy."*
>
> *~Peter Shaffer*

end of the path, greet the King with confidence and with a thankful heart, because He alone made the journey possible and the destination wonderful.

Fantasy reflects life. That is the connection that I felt early on, and that is what makes stories of adventure and imagination so timeless and valuable. Should a person stay away from fantasy fiction altogether to avoid the dangers and pitfalls that sometimes come with it? You could, but you'd be missing an excellent training opportunity for LIFE. And that's a forest through which we must all travel.

Chapter I
The Hero's Journey: What We Can Learn from the Ultimate Epic Adventure

"The hero is one who kindles a great light in the world, who sets up blazing torches in the dark streets of life for men to see by." ~Felix Adler

We all know about dark times, or at least think we do.

We are mindful of personal loss, tragedy, and anguish. We understand perfectly well the hopelessness that sometimes wells up inside our souls, when it seems that life itself is too great a burden to bear. Sometimes we feel utterly crushed beneath the weight of circumstances that are beyond our control.

Apply even an ounce of humanity to a study of history, and the horrific darkness will take your breath away. Imagine the terror and indescribable suffering of the Jews in World War II. Or the men and women of Africa who were taken from their families and crammed into the bellies of cargo ships with death and decay all around them. Or the Christians living in hiding in pagan Rome, daily watching as friends and loved ones were captured and taken to the arena for torture and death. The details of any of these historical circumstances are too grisly to imagine, nor do I wish to relate them here.

We look at the world today and all the darkness that still exists, oozing up through the cracks of "civilized" society; in the news, on the television, even in our own communities.

We know there are dark times ahead.

What will sustain us, and our children, when the last vestiges of all that is good and pure and right are finally swept away? How can we teach our young people courage, loyalty, selflessness, perseverance, and compassion in a world so dominated by hatred, greed, and malice?

> *"Lo, the hosts of evil round us scorn the Christ, assail His ways! ...Grant us wisdom, grant us courage, for the living of these days."*
>
> *~ Harry Emerson Fosdick: God of Grace and God of Glory*

We must show them.

There is a kind of story that has been around for thousands of years. It has survived through all the darkness of the ages as a beacon of light, giving life and hope to those in the shadow of the most terrible evil. It is a story of pain, suffering, and sacrifice. It is the story of a Hero, and what he must do to save those who cannot save themselves. The odds are overwhelmingly stacked against him, but he pushes forward despite temptation, pain and fear. And in the end, when the dust settles on the last field of battle, the forces of darkness are driven far from the land. Light returns in a glorious new dawn that promises life and happiness to all those who had been crushed by wickedness.

This story is God's gift to us, and it is our only weapon against the powers of darkness.

Where did the "Hero's Journey" idea come from?

During my freshman year of college, one of my professors, Dr. Jenny Mueller-Roebke, introduced me to "The Hero's Journey" literary motif. I connected immediately. All the stories that were so important to me growing up and all the books that really "stuck" with me were really versions of this one ancient pattern.

You see, since the fall of creation, mankind has had this concept indelibly imprinted upon his heart. We are lost. There is a giant cosmic evil that is spreading over our world, and we are powerless to stop it. Sin, death, and the Devil are simply too strong for any of us. We need a Hero.

All of the most profound literary feats throughout the ages have been inspired by this, the greatest story of all time. Jesus Christ comes as the Hero, sacrificing Himself to accomplish what we could not do for ourselves. And in a strange, amazing way, this story becomes our own as we learn what it means to live out the life of a Christian warrior, battling the forces of evil in our own hearts and in the world around us.

Any "Hero's Journey" story is a worthwhile read and a great way to learn the most valuable lessons in life. We see actions that are noble, pure and good modeled for us. We learn how to act in the face of doubt, fear, pain, confusion, loneliness, and temptation. We see the best of humanity come forward when people are really put to the test. The world of fantasy is host to a tremendous number of fantastic stories about admirable heroes.

This chapter will point out many of the common elements in "Hero's Journey" stories and explain how they relate to the life of a Christian. Unfortunately, the forces of darkness in our world are attacking and undermining even this age-old, divinely inspired paradigm. Some literature today aims to twist and pervert the classic patterns so that they better fit the secular philosophies of our age, so I will also caution and advise readers on some of the ways that this typically occurs. As you read, you may find opportunities to test some of the books and movies with which you are already familiar!

"Old heroes have never died. They are only sleeping at the bottom of our mind, waiting for our call. We have need for them. They represent the wisdom of our race." ~Stanley Kunitz

1. There is an unknown evil force at work in the world...

In nearly every Hero's Journey story, life is relatively peaceful for the hero and his or her friends, relatives, community, etc. People are blissfully ignorant of some powerful malevolent force at work to enslave or destroy their village, their kingdom, or oftentimes the whole world. At times they know about the evil, but it doesn't really affect them because it is distant and they feel that it really isn't a threat or concern of theirs.

The hero is no exception to this. He or she is not a hero yet, but an ordinary person living an ordinary life. All of that is about to change suddenly and irrevocably when the hero is forced from the "ordinary world" and initiated into a dangerous *new* world.

In some stories, the hero leaves the ordinary life because he discovers the existence of the powerful evil, or learns that the threat is more immediate than anyone realizes. Sometimes he tries to convince others of this, only to be mocked and scorned. Other times, the hero is forced out of the comfortable life of ease and peacefulness still not knowing much (if anything) about the evil forces lurking in the new world he is about to enter. Either way, the hero never grasps at this point just how great a magnitude of evil he is up against. Sometimes heroes foolishly believe that they can handle whatever is coming their way, and are in for a major surprise.

Application to Christian Life

We know all too well that when life is good, it's easy to forget about the darkness that is out there in our world. Even in the best of times, we are surrounded by people still in Satan's grasp; those who do not know Jesus Christ as their Lord and Savior. They are perishing, and they don't even realize it. *We* know it, but the knowledge doesn't always seem to be of immediate concern. It is a far off, distant threat, like the evil Empire in the Star Wars saga. Yes, it's out there, but we've plenty of time to deal with that later (exactly how and when we could never say). Or we may even be afraid of being mocked and scorned when we try to warn others of the evil that is out there, threatening to devour them, so we just stay put.

Another thing we can learn from this part of the Hero's Journey motif is how to handle our own "separation from the ordinary world." Most of us have experienced times in life when our whole world is turned upside down in a few short days, or even hours. How do we react? To whom do we turn? Hero's Journey stories are easy for us to relate to because we can identify with the "hero in crisis" who isn't really a hero yet, nor are they sure they ever will be. The path ahead is hidden from us, and we've no idea of the enormity of what's out there. And generally speaking, there's no going back.

Sometimes we really think we know what we're up against and try to take it on all by ourselves. This is dangerous at best, and downright stupid when we stop to think about all the help that we have at our disposal as Christians; faithful friends, spouses, pastors, and of course God Himself.

This "I can handle it myself" mentality is especially dangerous on a spiritual level, for several reasons. First of all, Satan is a much more powerful adversary than any of us realize (see the Hero's Journey connection?). He's been around perfecting his craft for thousands of years. We generally fail miserably when we try to take him on all by ourselves. When faced with temptation, we need the help of those around us, we *need* the Word of God as a weapon and a sure defense, and we *need* Jesus Christ to restore us to our Heavenly Father when we fail.

That is where we can really get ourselves into trouble; when we try to tackle our salvation all on our own. Satan loves it when we do this, and he is always trying to lure us into this trap. So many people believe that they can somehow live a good enough life and be a good enough person to earn their own way into heaven. Sorry folks, but we're not *that* Hero. While we certainly have our own battles to fight (and plenty of them), Jesus is the only one who will ever go head to head with Satan, live

> *"If you…presume to still your conscience with your contrition and penance, you will never obtain peace of mind, but will have to despair in the end. If we allow sin to remain in our conscience and try to deal with it there…it will be much too strong for us and will live on forever. But if we behold it resting on Christ and overcome by his resurrection…it is dead and nullified."*
>
> *~Martin Luther*

7

the perfect life, and triumph over sin and death. He's the only One who ever *could* do this, being free from the curse of original sin. All others who try are destined to fail. Trusting in our own powers for salvation leads only to despair and ultimately death.

Danger!

A word of caution about an alarming trend in modern fantasy fiction: be sure that your Hero's Journey story portrays bad as bad and good as good. Whatever the powerful evil that is threatening the kingdom/world/universe, make sure that it is black and white, especially for young readers. Morality itself is under heavy attack in the secular world today. "Evil" is often no longer even acknowledged as a reality. So instead of good vs. evil, you end up with a contest of wills, with two groups who have opposing goals and desires but neither of which is really "right" or "wrong" in any way (lest we offend anyone). This ethical "gray area" aims to weaken the authority of God's Word, and anyone who opposes this muddled philosophy is labeled "intolerant" or "unaccepting."

This moral "gray area" has also given a lot of momentum to the idea that "the end justifies the means." Much of the literature that is available to young people today teaches them that any methods are acceptable (given the right circumstances) to defeat their adversary. The basic idea is that good is really only good some of the time, and evil can sometimes be "good" when used in a given situation. These "situational ethics" are merely a product of the erosion of absolute right and wrong, and are a serious threat to society. In the words of Christopher Dawson, "As soon as men decide that all means are permitted to fight an evil, then their good becomes indistinguishable from the evil that they set out to destroy."

Another frightening trend in modern Hero's Journey stories is the portrayal of the Church or some other authority figure as the "evil" that the hero is up against. We live in a sinful, fallen world, and corruption certainly takes place in all parts of society from the family to government and even within the Christian church. It's okay to acknowledge that fact, and the training of a young Christian warrior wouldn't be complete without equipping them with the ability to confront and deal with that situation if it arises. But what we're seeing more and more of late are atheistic authors who are disgruntled with religion trying to encourage young readers to reject the Church's teachings as false. And by doing so through literature, they are being extremely effective. It's a sneaky, underhanded way to get kids to question the Bible, their parents, and any other authority in their life simply because they *are* an authority.

It shouldn't surprise us, though. The philosophy of today is generally summed up by, "Live for yourself; don't let anyone tell you what to do or what's right or wrong." Sadly, this mantra couldn't be further away from the real message that the classic Hero's Journey stories have always taught; live for others. Do what you *know* is right, even when it isn't easy.

So be on your guard. What should be a wonderful teaching tool for young Christians is also being used as a brain-washing tactic by secular humanist authors. The good news is that this tactic is usually pretty easy to identify, since the authors are more concerned with promoting an ideology than telling a great story. Watch for it in the books and movies you read, preview materials that your kids are reading, and warn others when you find these toxic ideas in what appear to be otherwise wholesome stories.

2. The hero is generally "unlikely" and has a certain "innocent" quality

God uses the most unlikely people imaginable to achieve great things. Look at old, tongue-tied Moses, or little David, or the murderer Saul. The heroes are always the type that you'd least expect. Instead of some prince or warrior, the one to save the world will be small, poor, insignificant, and oftentimes very young. Of course, young heroes are easier for young readers to identify with, but they also remind the rest of us that great things come in small packages.

The point is, the hero will rise from humble beginnings. Or sometimes, the hero *will* be a prince or a warrior, but they are brought low by some catastrophe or extreme misfortune, only to rise once more from the mists of obscurity. After all, not many of us can easily relate to princes and warriors, but we *can* relate to ordinary folks who seem to get caught up over their heads in something beyond their control.

No matter the size, shape, age, or position of the hero, he or she will always have a certain innocence at the beginning of the journey. Sometimes that innocence is a burden, getting them into trouble because they lack the skills or experience needed to survive in the new world they've been flung into. But usually, it is their innocence, their code of ethics, their child-like faith that sets them apart in the new world. It is something they cherish, knowing that it separates them from the forces of evil that they are fighting against (refer to above quote by Christopher Dawson).

> *"Childhood ends when we realize that Santa Claus is make-believe, and the monster in the closet is for real."*
>
> *~Robert Brault*

Is the hero able to retain that special "innocent" quality? Yes and no. Generally, the hero does hold fast to their beliefs and principles. But there is a certain part of their innocent nature that will certainly be lost. It is the part of the hero that allowed them to believe that the world was basically good, that people were generally kind, that nature is typically benevolent. It is the part of the hero that had been sheltered from pain, death, sorrow, and cruelty. This part of their innocence is tragically and brutally destroyed, and can never be mended. It reflects a sad fact of life; that our children must ultimately grow up and face the world for what it really is. There will come a time when the hero must leave the safety of the ordinary world and begin their journey, and life will never be the same. Time and time again, heroes have discovered that they can't just pick up the pieces and go back to their old life again, because they aren't the same person as they were before the journey began.

Application to Christian Life

This is the part of the story that can take us from, "Who, me?" to "Here am I, send me!" When God calls us to task, our initial reaction is always to find someone else who is better or more qualified than we are. We don't *want* to leave the ordinary world. It's comfy. Besides, God must be mistaken if He chose a nobody like me for this task.

> *"Grace is given to heal the spiritually sick, not to decorate spiritual heroes."*
>
> *~Martin Luther*

We can think of a million reasons why we shouldn't go. But God sends us anyway. "But I'm not prepared for the journey!" God says, "Go. I'll equip you along the way." The thing is, God is smarter than we are. We don't even know what we know. God *has* been equipping you for the journey, only the journey is probably going to be something very different from what you're expecting. You'll start to see, when the time comes, how your gracious Heavenly Father has prepared you in His own special way for the challenges that lie ahead. You might not feel like a warrior or prince, but maybe a warrior or prince wouldn't be the right person for this task. Whatever it is, it was given especially to *you*, and that should give you some measure of confidence as you head out on your way.

So what about this whole "innocence" thing? I know what you're thinking; "I'm not innocent! I've been bad, bad, bad!" Understand that we're not talking about a moral innocence here. After all, we were conceived in sin, under the curse of a fallen world. "Innocent" simply refers to our understanding of the way the world really is, as explained above.

You might have felt sometimes like you "wish you didn't know now what you didn't know then." Perhaps you can identify a specific instance or moment when your illusion of the world and human nature came crashing down. Horrible, tragic things happen to heroes along their journey; things they never imagined possible before leaving the "ordinary world". These are things that, sadly, can never be "unlearned" or erased from our memories. This personal, permanent change is just another part of the repercussions of sin in the world, and there is no going back to the way things were before.

> *"My comfort in my suffering is this:*
> *Your promise preserves my life."*
>
> *~Psalm 119:50*

The test for a Christian is really a matter of whether we lose the other part of our "innocence" at the same time. Do we let the evil in the world destroy what sets us apart as children of God? Or, like the heroes of our stories, do we cling ever more closely to the values and beliefs that set us apart? This is a challenge for every Christian, and it isn't a one-time test. The world never ceases to shock me with its cruelty and sadness. Just when I thought I'd seen it all, I watch the evening news and see some new heart-rending tragedy caused by humanity's wickedness. It makes a person simply want to give up on the whole human race. But that's part of the evil we're fighting against ("The dragon is everywhere; it is a part of you"- see #21).

Danger!

From a literary standpoint, everything is riding on the hero. Of course, they are certainly allowed to have their character flaws (and are actually expected to). But it is the hero who is the crux of the story, and who is serving as the reader's model. If the character is *too* flawed, young readers (well, any reader actually) can come away with a very distorted message. Yet this is exactly what is becoming more common in some modern Hero's Journey stories.

Traditionally, the hero or heroine of the story stands up for what is good and right, even when they will suffer for doing so. After all, that's the kind of behavior we want to model for our children and ourselves, right? And when the hero does make a poor choice, there is some kind of consequence as a result of this sinful action (just as there would be in real life). The hero regrets his mistake and works diligently to correct whatever injustice has been caused as a result of his lapse of judgment. He's not perfect, but he takes responsibility for his own actions. And again, generally speaking, the hero is the one to stand up for truth, justice, and morality when these values are under attack.

And yet, we are seeing many stories today with young "heroic" characters who seem to be above the law or any sense of personal responsibility. If you need something along your journey, steal it. After all, "the end justifies the means." If someone wronged you, take revenge. Do whatever feels right to you, and don't let anyone else tell you what's right or wrong. Are you starting to see a pattern emerge here?

I would also like to caution readers about a recent phenomenon called the "anti-hero." This character started as a "rogue" type of good guy, your Robin Hood or Dirty Harry kind of hero. While they don't always follow the rules, they have basically good intentions in the long run (can you see the slippery slope here?). This kind of hero is, naturally, appealing to human nature. My nature wants to do whatever I feel like. It wants complete freedom from authority and control. It wants to rebel.

Well, now the "anti-hero" has gotten to the point where the villain of the story is the one audiences are rooting for. In "The

Dark Knight", Batman's strict code of ethics puts him at second fiddle to the Joker, whose nihilistic/anarchist ideals give him total freedom from all moral, legal and societal constraints. Not surprisingly, audience members find this appealing and he becomes the "closet hero" of millions of teenagers and adults across the country.

Several of my students a few years ago were discussing how much they liked the young Tom Riddle (Voldemort-to-be) in one of the Harry Potter stories. I was taken aback, and pointed out that he was absolutely evil, twisted, and maniacal, and how could anyone admire that sort of thing? They responded, "Exactly. He's got that 'bad-boy' thing going on where he can do *whatever he wants*." I shudder just recollecting the incident, especially when I recall that the first commandment of Satanism is "Do as thou wilt."

To be fair to Rowling, I do not believe that the Harry Potter books portray Tom Riddle as an admirable character by any stretch of the imagination, and Harry is generally a hero who stands up for what is true and good (with a few notable exceptions...). But that makes the incident all the more frightening. This secular/ Satanic philosophy of "do your own thing" is so entrenched in the minds of young people that they will, consciously or subconsciously, turn the villains into heroes. And to be honest, there are some unsavory authors out there who intentionally lay this trap in front of them.

Because so much is riding on the heroes of these stories, we need to make absolutely certain that they are exhibiting the kind of behavior that we want to be emulating. And therein lies the final application of this element to Christian life: What kind of hero will *you* be on your own journey? You would be shocked to learn just how much is riding on you. Friends, coworkers, children, neighbors; they all see the kind of life you live, and it is a testament to your faith. For good or ill, you are representing Christ when you adopt His name as a Christian. Be sure that your own heroes are Christ-like. Remember that people tend to become whatever they pretend to be. You may not feel much like a hero, but you can pretend to be one without being labeled a hypocrite. In fact, you're *called* to do it.

> *"The hero is valorous because he stands up to every threat directed against his values. Heroism requires value conflict."*
>
> ~Andrew Bernstein

3. There is something special or unknown about the hero's lineage or past

So there's this kid who is growing up in a small village with his parents, but what he doesn't know is that they aren't actually his real parents because his real parents are the king and queen who gave him into the protection of a lowly peasant shortly before being killed by the evil invaders from across the sea and if anyone finds out that their only child is still alive it would be an all-out manhunt for his head on a silver platter.

Sound familiar? While this element of the Hero's Journey can easily become clichéd, it does serve an important role in the motif as a whole (and most writers do a much better job of incorporating it into their story than the example above would suggest). The hero has a distinct duality to their own nature; they are weak, poor, lowly, or "unlikely" in some way, but at the same time they are somehow very special or unique. Perhaps they have hidden powers, or royal ancestry, or parents of special prominence (often even a god or goddess in mythology). Whatever it is, heroes are usually completely oblivious to their own unique heritage. If they do know, it usually matters about as much to them as the vague threat of an evil empire on the other side of the galaxy; and even then they rarely know the whole extent of their own background.

Someday, the hero will learn about his past, his parents, or his exceptional identity. For now, it is precisely *not* knowing that gives the hero the innocence, the good nature, and the humility that he needs for survival and development as a true hero. After all, being a hero is about more than just waving a sword around. It is about having a pure heart and noble mind. It is about standing firmly and bravely in the face of danger. It is about rising above the evil all around and being willing to sacrifice your own good for the sake of others. If the hero knew what a hot-shot he was born to be, he would probably have such a snobby, arrogant, entitled attitude that there would be virtually no chance that he would ever become the type of person to go out of his way to help someone else.

Samples of this element abound throughout the ages. In Homer's *Odyssey*, Telemachos must learn how to defend his besieged home and mother without the help or advice of his absent father. He is forced to strike out on his own, gaining the confidence and abilities he will need to eventually stand by his father in the end and prove himself, at last, the true son of royal Odysseus. Had his father been at home, his journey and subsequent growth would have never occurred; he would have missed out on the opportunity to develop such noble attributes, and ironically may have fallen miserably short of achieving the identity of "his father's son."

King Arthur grew up as a squire in the service of a common knight, not knowing anything about his royal father or mother. In his day, being a great king meant being a great knight; the ruler must understand better than anyone else the laws of chivalry. It doesn't take a real Merlin to figure out that it's a whole lot easier to teach a *squire* the values of knighthood than it is to teach the same thing to a spoiled *prince*.

In today's literature, every character from Harry Potter to Luke Skywalker to Bilbo Baggins has something special or unknown about their past at the beginning of their journey. Finding out what that missing piece is and making it a reality for themselves is a vital part of the hero's journey.

Application to Christian Life

"Okay," you're thinking, "but you can't possibly believe that every one of *us* has something special about our past or identity. There are only so many princes and princesses running around in the world!" Ah, but we have a piece of our heritage that is much more special than any ancestry or inherited mystical powers could ever be.

We are the adopted children of the King, and heirs to all the riches of the most powerful Ruler in the universe. We are His children, and don't doubt for a moment that He is taking a very special interest in *your* journey! The King is on your side, and when you get into trouble on the dark forest paths, all you have to do is call for help. His guards will leap from the battlements of His palace, soar into the air with a dazzling burst of light, and descend upon your foes with fiery swords. How *cool* is it to know

> *"Call upon me in the day of trouble; I will deliver you, and you will honor me."*
>
> *~Psalm 50:15*

that your Father has that kind of firepower and more at His disposal?! You see, you're not just the son of a god, like the heroes of the Greek myths; we are sons and daughters of The One True God.

The problem is, this part of our identity *is* unknown to us, at least at the start of our journey. We are told the information plainly at our baptism, and reminded of it often as we go to church and study the Bible. But for some reason we just don't seem to get it. It isn't a *reality* to us yet.

We're like the peasant kid growing up in the village, whose mom keeps telling him that his father is really the king and someday he'll come back for us and we'll all live together in the palace forever. Despite the fact that the mother's story is absolutely true, the child will respond in one of two ways, similar to the way Christians respond to the "ho-hum" fact that God is their Father.

The first type of Christian is like the peasant child who would like to believe it's true, but figures it's just a story that mom made up to make herself and me feel better about our present situation. Sadly, when this person sets off through the forest and is beset by deadly foes, he never looks up to the castle ramparts and calls for help, because he thinks it would be foolish to believe in such a fantasy.

The second type of Christian is like the peasant child who listens to his mother's stories, *knows* that they are true, but just doesn't see how it matters for him in his life. In fact, it often breeds bitterness and resentment in his heart. "Here I am slopping pigs and working hard and starving, and my father is up there in his palace watching it all! Doesn't he care?!" How many times have thoughts like this crossed your own mind? The truth is, the King does see His child suffering and laboring, and it pains Him deeply. He sorrows over the separation that has been caused by sin, and yearns for the day of our reunion. And He is always ready at a moment's notice to send help when we call out to Him, and His heart leaps every time we cast our eyes upon His dwelling.

Remember that God did not cause the separation that brings so much daily turmoil into our lives. It was His sacrifice of life that set us free in the first place, when He sent His only begotten Son to our crummy little village so that He might become The Path through the forest of life; the only Way that leads to the Father. Remember that, like Telemachos and Arthur and Harry, our present trials and sufferings will one day enable us to stand and fight boldly in the face of overwhelming danger. Each step of the journey, we realize a little more of our own special identity, and become a little more like our Father.

Danger!

How can such a wonderful, beautiful literary element hold any danger to a Christian reader? Well, believe it or not, not every Hero's Journey story out there today utilizes this element in such noble and admirable fashion. Perhaps, as I mentioned at the beginning of this section, some authors feel that this element is too clichéd and makes the story too "predictable," so they are more inclined to "think outside the box" when it comes the hero's past. Maybe it's simply for shock value, or a sense of avant-garde literary artistry. Whatever the reason, many stories today that would otherwise follow the classic Hero's Journey pattern now exclude this element (which is too bad), or invert it (which is worse).

I think the scariest way that this element has been tampered with is the inversion where the hero discovers a part of their past or identity that is *not* true. They discover that their father is not who he said he was, or that something they thought was a special part of their heritage was a lie, or they uncover some horrific secret about their family's past. Granted, these are all situations that very well *could* affect the real life of a Christian, and they can be written in a way that addresses the issue and deals with it in an edifying manner. But more often, this inversion is used by the same anti-religious authors who simply want to cause fear, doubt and suspicion in the minds of young people about anyone they respect and anything they've been taught. Use your own discretion and judgment.

One other possible danger is that heroes often have a special part of their identity or heritage that is reflective of a pagan belief system. They possess magical abilities, or are a descendant of a certain god or goddess, or are actually a reincarnation of someone from the past. I'm reluctant to rule out *every* story that contains such elements as possible reading material for Christians, because usually the inclusion of that element serves a distinct purpose and is far enough removed from "reality" that it presents no real danger to the reader (this is more thoroughly explained in Chapter 2). If fact, it often serves to reinforce some of the very faith concepts we've been discussing.

Magic is very commonplace in fantasy stories, and it generally doesn't present a threat unless there is link to "real-world" witchcraft (i.e. detailed spells and rituals); otherwise I think it highly unlikely that anyone will abandon their faith on the belief that they've inherited ambiguous magical powers. But do be on guard for Wicca, Satanic rituals, Shamanism, Voodoo, and Eastern Mysticism, as these all have a presence in our communities (it's true) and present a clear and present danger especially to young Christians.

Similarly, stories with heroes who have gods or goddesses for parents/grandparents/etc. usually don't strike me as particularly dangerous except perhaps to some very young readers. Greek and Roman mythology are pretty much on par with fairy tales these days, and I haven't personally heard of any cases of Christians converting to the worship of Greek gods solely because they read a story about one. Greek mythology simply doesn't have the presence in our society as a "faith" to present much of a danger to young people. Stories of Greek mythology often serve as fables, teaching ethics and morality and can sometimes even act as strong parables for Christian concepts (again, *sometimes*).

However, I get very nervous when dealing with any form of reincarnation as a basis for the "unknown past or lineage" element. New Age religions and Eastern Mysticism are growing by leaps and bounds in our society, and they are extremely dangerous ideologies – both spiritually and socially. Practitioners of these faiths are experts at making their religion palatable to Christians. It *seems* so harmless, and they link individual concepts and elements from Christianity to their belief system, so that it almost becomes a blend. Many Christians who leave the Church for these organizations still believe that they are "Christians," and would label themselves as such. But don't be fooled; there is no room for Jesus or the Gospel with them. Like all false religions and empty ideologies, it is simply another branch of Satanism, sprung up in new form. I'm afraid that most books utilizing these concepts, even Hero's Journey stories, will do more harm than good, especially to young readers and new Christians.

4. The hero experiences a distinct "Call to Adventure"

Sooner or later, the hero experiences a wake-up call, and sometimes it can be a very rude awakening. Often this is when the hero first becomes aware of the powerful evil that threatens the community, but sometimes it occurs even before they discover what's lurking out there. Many times, the hero even begins the journey accidentally or involuntarily. However it occurs, there is a precise moment where the hero first feels pushed or compelled to leave the "ordinary world" behind.

If the hero sets out with purpose, it will usually change before long. They never realize the full extent of what they are getting into or just what they're up against. This is Frodo saying, "I just need to take the ring to the village of Bree, then my adventure will be over." Yeah, right. Or it is Willow saying, "If I can only take the baby safely to the Dikini crossroads, I'll be able to go back to my normal life." Fat chance. Or it might be Luke Skywalker saying, "Look, I can take you as far as Anchorhead. You can get a transport there to Mos Eisley or wherever you're going." Keep dreaming, pal.

Again, the problem is that the ordinary world is so warm and cozy that setting out on the adventure is a lot like getting out of bed on a cold morning. Even for heroes who already feel a "general" call to adventure – that is, an urge for something new and different and exciting – even for them, it's difficult to want to just jump in with both feet. And if they *really* knew what they were getting into, they'd probably run in the opposite direction.

That's why it's almost a blessing when the hero doesn't have any choice in the matter. The call to adventure could come in the form of a group of thugs throwing the hero into a van and kidnapping him. Or perhaps the hero returns to his small village to find it in smoldering ruins. Or a wizard and a group of dwarves come barging into his living room and make themselves at home. The point is, the hero is almost never *looking* for an adventure, but the adventure seems to find him anyway.

Application to Christian Life

The concept of being "called" to something in life should be no mystery to a Christian. God calls us to all kinds of walks in life, whether it's vocation, friendship, family responsibilities, or any other venture. God is always pushing us forward, and we always tend to drag our heels. God says, "Go. Be strong and courageous," and we say, "But...!" Part of becoming a hero of the faith is learning how to recognize the call to adventure and how to respond appropriately.

God is calling us constantly. There are always small things that we are called to do; helping a stranded motorist, aiding a frantic coworker, or providing a word of encouragement to someone struggling with their own journey. God calls in big ways, too; all the way up to "The Call" to go and serve Him in the ministry. Just remember that whether it's big or small or anywhere in between, it is all part of your "calling" as a Christian, and it is part of your own "hero's journey." We don't know where we're headed or the full extent of what we're getting into, but God does. His Word will be a Lamp unto our feet and a Light unto our path, showing us the next step all along the way.

What a mercy it really is that, like the heroes of many stories, sometimes we don't have any choice in the matter. We suddenly find ourselves being whirled around in a chaotic frenzy of change and activity that is outside of our control! How did this happen to me?! Relax. God is good, and whatever is happening isn't an accident, and it isn't a coincidence. Things may be pretty uncomfortable for a while, but pay attention and you'll see how God is leading and equipping you for what's ahead. Just keep your feet fitted with the readiness that comes from the gospel of peace, and keep the Sword of the Spirit at your fingertips, and God will get you through it.

> *"Fight the good fight with all your might; Christ is your strength, and Christ your right. Lay hold on life, and it shall be your joy and crown eternally."*
>
> *"Run the straight race through God's good grace; lift up your eyes, and seek His face. Life with its way before us lies; Christ is the path, and Christ the prize."*
>
> *~John S.B. Monsell: Fight the Good Fight*

5. The hero must make a "crossroads decision"

It's a part of life. It happens to everyone. It happened to Robert Frost:

"Two roads diverged in a yellow wood,
And sorry I could not travel both
And be one traveler, long I stood
And looked down one as far as I could
To where it bent in the undergrowth;

Then took the other, as just as fair,
And having perhaps the better claim,
Because it was grassy and wanted wear;
Though as for that the passing there
Had worn them really about the same,

And both that morning equally lay
In leaves no step had trodden black.
Oh, I kept the first for another day!
Yet knowing how way leads on to way,
I doubted if I should ever come back.

I shall be telling this with a sigh
Somewhere ages and ages hence:
Two roads diverged in a wood, and I-
I took the one less traveled by,
And that has made all the difference."
~The Road Not Taken

Sooner or later, the hero is going to be faced with a decision to make, and it will be a decision that will affect the rest of his life. The tricky part is that the decision doesn't usually seem all that significant at the time. Should I walk home or take a cab? Should I go to the gym today or hit the beach? Should I turn around and go back to the restaurant and look for my hat? The decision generally doesn't strike the hero as something that is going to affect the outcome of the rest of their life. Yet the choice they make precipitates some crisis that majorly impacts the direction of their journey.

What would have happened if I had chosen the other "path"? There is no way to know. Remember that the Hero's Journey reflects life. It is a one-way path, and just as in Frost's poem, you will never get a chance to find out where the other path would have led.

There is a tremendous amount of responsibility on the hero to make the right choices. But often, both paths lay equally fair ahead, and the hero labors to look down one as far as he can to try and determine the outcome. It always seems to bend into the undergrowth not far ahead, however, and the hero is left to decide (or not, which is also a decision) which path to take and make the best decision that he can.

> "It's not hard to make decisions when you know what your values are."
>
> ~Roy Disney

Crossroads decisions can happen at any point along the hero's journey, not just right at the start. There could be only one conspicuous "crossroads," or there could be several along the way. As the hero grows, so too does their ability to make wise choices and discern subtle advantages in the paths that they follow.

Application to Christian Life

Christians have many choices that they must make in life. Thankfully, faith is not one of them. We certainly make choices about going to church and reading the Bible, and our faith grows or diminishes accordingly. But it is the Holy Spirit who brings us to faith – a miracle quite outside of our own powers. Thanks be to God that He has reached out to me through the saving power of the Gospel and made me His child forever!

God gives us many opportunities to make choices in our lives. He isn't a "Fate Machine" – laying out our lives in black and white, winding us up, and forcing us to follow the dotted line. Oh, He certainly *knows* exactly what choices I'll make along the way. He absolutely *guides* me in which choices would be pleasing to Him and most beneficial for my life, but ultimately He leaves many of the decisions up to my own free will. And I also think that there are some "crossroads decisions" in our lives with multiple God-pleasing directions. Here, God sees both possible futures, promises to be with me down whichever path I take, and works His good and gracious will for the benefit of all in either case.

When we are faced with difficult decisions in life and stressed out by the knowledge that "way leads on to way" and that we will never get a chance to come back and travel the other path, we have a sure and steady guide. Pray to your Heavenly Father for wisdom and direction. Turn to His Word and let Him speak to you through Holy Scripture. If God says, "Go this way," then go with courage and faith. If not, don't be dismayed. God loves you enough to let you make some of your own choices throughout your journey. If both paths are God-pleasing and in accordance with His Word, then choose the one that's "grassy and wanted wear," or the one with the smoother surface, or the one that looks more interesting. Go whichever way you please, and God will lead and bless you and present you with all manner of challenges to overcome and people to minister to.

> *"Sometimes the road less traveled is less traveled for a reason."*
>
> *~Jerry Seinfeld*

Danger!

Here it comes again, the "Go your own way, do your own thing" mentality. I know, I know; I just finished saying that sometimes God lets us choose our own path in life. That's true, but I also said that we must first make sure that path is in accordance with His will. Granted, we can still choose to go down a path that we *know* is *not* in accordance with God's will (and we often do!), but rest assured that it will end up in trouble and hardship. God knows the destinations of *all* the winding paths of this life, and He often leads us down trails that are difficult at first but conclude with green pastures and gentle waters. We choose for ourselves the trails that look smooth and wide, but terminate in cliffs, mires, or wolves' dens.

> *"There are two kinds of people: those who say to God, "Thy will be done," and those to whom God says, "All right, then, have it your way."*
>
> ~C.S. Lewis

The dominant message for young people today is that they should do "whatever they feel like," regardless of what advice or instruction has been given to them by parents, teachers, pastors, or especially Scripture. Instead of encouraging us to seek Godly advice, society teaches us to obey our "instincts." In fact, a main tenet of modern philosophy is to do exactly the *opposite* of what mom, dad, or God tells you to do simply because it *is* different (a terrible misinterpretation of Frost's taking "the road less traveled by"). After all, you don't want to be like everybody else, do you? Ironically, it is only the elite minority who even attempt to live a Godly life, and the vast majority rebel against God's will under the guise of being "unique."

Watch the heroes of your stories carefully and judge their crossroads decisions with a critical eye. If they make poor choices, do they learn from their mistakes? Do they suffer consequences? Try to discern what philosophy is being promoted by this book to you and your children; a model of Godly wisdom or an example of reckless rebellion.

6. Future events are foreshadowed

Heroes are often given some kind of warning or glimpse of things that haven't yet come to pass. Perhaps there is a sign of danger up ahead, or a "chance" occurrence that signals something positive around the next corner. Why? Well, from a literary standpoint, it creates excitement and tension for the reader, as well a sense of irony. But more importantly, it draws attention to an important real-life issue: Trying to peer into the unknown. Being perceptive to subtle cues and bits of wisdom can help us to make good choices when we come to a crossroads. But even events that have been foreshadowed rarely play out like we expected them to.

Foreshadowing most often occurs in three main forms: dreams, omens, and prophecies. "Heralds" announce things that are about to occur, or that are occurring right now, or that happened in the past in another location. Often heralds are people – individuals – but sometimes they can be objects such as letters, monuments, devices, etc. "Harbingers" predict doom and typically take the form of dreams, objects, or unnatural/supernatural phenomena.

Many Hero's Journey stories involve a dream that predicts or foreshadows something. Sometimes the dream reveals something to the hero, like the threat of a powerful evil force or a significant detail about the hero's past or lineage. Oftentimes, the hero is reluctant to take action based on the dream, because after all, it was probably "just a dream."

Omens tend to be more powerful motivators, especially because they are frequently coupled with a dream. A hero might have a dream about a giant black stone with strange runes carved into it, but when that same stone appears in the middle of town overnight, it becomes hard to ignore. The hero probably doesn't know exactly what it means yet, but it's usually clear whether the omen bodes good or ill. Sometimes the journey begins simply as a quest to find answers about the omen itself.

Prophecies are the clearest and most common form of foreshadowing in fantasy fiction, and especially in Hero's Journey stories. Quite often there will be a prophecy linked to the hero's unknown or special past. Sometimes, the prophecy itself *is* the thing that is special about the hero's past.

Heroes have a difficult time of it when they are told that they are the "Chosen One," the "Child of Promise," or some such foreboding title. It may well be that the discovery of this information is what spurs the hero to set out on their journey, either to fulfill the prophecy…or to escape it.

Prophecies also have a strong tendency to be "self-fulfilling." Let's say that upon turning fifteen years old our hero learns that when she was born, the village elder announced that the strange birthmark on her left foot indicated that she would be the one to overthrow the invaders from across the sea. Terrified (she's just a normal girl, after all), she flees to a different country where she discovers a knight who turns out to be her father. Her mother was shipwrecked in the village where the girl was born and died after giving birth, so dad presumed they were both lost at sea. Two years pass. Dad goes to fight in a war to the east (he's a knight, remember), and is captured by the ruthless leader of the enemy. The girl embarks on an epic quest to rescue her father, having many adventures and defeating the barbarian leader in the process, causing the remaining barbarians to flee back across the sea. On the way home, the girl stops in a familiar fishing village and is hailed the Heroine of the Prophecy.

> "A person often meets his destiny on the road he took to avoid it."
>
> ~Jean de La Fontaine

Now, of course, the question is: If the prophecy was never made, would the girl have ever left the village in the first place? If not, would she ever have been reunited with her father and spurred on toward her epic quest which eventually led to the defeat of the barbarian invaders? Or did the prophecy's very existence *cause* it to come true? Don't spend *too* much time thinking it over. But it is worthwhile to consider the significance of this classic pattern as we think about the predictions we make for others and ourselves.

Application to Christian Life

If I'm always told that I'm worthless and that I'll never amount to anything, that's a pretty tough mold to break out of. The opinions of others mean a lot to us, especially those of parents, teachers, friends, and other people that we look up to and admire. Imagine, instead, if I'm told every day that I'm a child of God, and that He loves me enough to send His Son to die for me. Imagine if the people I love and admire all tell me that I'm destined to do great things, to help people – to be a hero.

> *"Dream lofty dreams, and as you dream, so you shall become. Your vision is the promise of what you shall one day be; your ideal is the prophecy of what you shall at last unveil."*
>
> ~James Allen

You see, there's nothing magical about how this works. We instinctively know which of those kids we would rather be. We *know* which one has a better chance at becoming the faith warrior that God wants him to be. The first kid was lied to his whole life, but after a while, that lie has a good chance of becoming a reality. The second kid grew up enveloped by the warm, wonderful truth; God loves me. What a difference that can make in the life of a child! What a difference it can make to *anyone*.

Danger!

Aren't we talking witchcraft, Voodoo, Shamanism? Aren't fortune tellers and mediums considered patently dangerous to the Christian faith? Well, you're right, and that's what this word of caution is all about.

Now before we start tearing pages out of any books, consider this: Dreams, omens, and prophecies *are* found in the Bible. God used them time and again to speak to His people and reveal His will to them. What we need to understand is that there is a difference between God taking the initiative and revealing Himself to someone through a dream, and us going out and consulting a medium to acquire some hidden knowledge.

Why doesn't God want us peering into the hidden mists of the future? I think for several reasons. One, He wants us to rely on *Him*. To live and walk by faith means to trust God to provide for what we need, and when we have questions we turn to Him in prayer. He reveals everything we need to know about His merciful will for us in Scripture. As we turn to other sources for answers, it betrays an already weak faith that will only get weaker as we remove ourselves from His strengthening Word. A right relationship with God will have us meeting the unknown challenges of each day, trusting in God to provide us with the strength we need to overcome them. We can always prepare for *whatever* lies around the next corner by studying the Bible and asking God to help us apply our hearts to wisdom.

Two, God knows what knowledge is good for us and what is bad for us. Why go looking for something that you know is going to be poisonous to your soul? It may very well be a mercy that we are spared knowing the details of what is about to come each day, because we would probably have a stress meltdown within the first week. And what kind of details are fortune tellers and mediums usually revealing to their "clients"? Almost exclusively bad news.

> *"For the household gods utter nonsense, and the diviners see lies; they tell false dreams and give empty consolation."*
>
> *~Zechariah 10:2*

Which brings me to reason number three: We can't force God to reveal anything to us that He desires to keep hidden, for those things belong to Him alone. Even a fortune teller doesn't have that power over God. So, let's see, where are the fortune tellers getting all of *their* information? That's right. Do you *really* want to start basing your future plans on information obtained from the Father of Lies? Why do you think mediums are so good at delivering bad news? The Devil delights in causing pain, sorrow, and despair in God's children.

Fortune telling is a seriously destructive and addictive vice. I don't like to see it appear in Hero's Journey stories as a method of foreshadowing, because it can be falsely portrayed in a positive light. The foreshadowing that occurs in classic Hero's Journey tales is mainly a literary device to advance the plot and can serve as a wonderful prompt for some critical thinking. But don't go looking for answers you weren't meant to know. Besides, chances are, the Devil understands how "self-fulfilling prophecies" work too, and be assured that he will use it to his advantage with any information he reveals to you.

7. "Threshold Guardians" try to prevent the hero from embarking on the quest

Yeah, the threshold; you know, the thing the bride gets carried across in the couple's new home. Every doorway has one, and we just walk all over them without thinking much about it. Well, the hero won't be crossing *any* thresholds on his way out the door without a little resistance.

"Threshold guardians" literally block the doorway so that the hero cannot leave and set out on the journey. Of course, many of them only have the best intentions at heart. Luke Skywalker's aunt and uncle try to stop him from leaving the farm because they know things that he doesn't. They don't want him to get hurt, so they try to keep him home to protect him. What they don't realize is that they are stopping him from becoming the hero that he was meant to be. But who can blame them? This kind of threshold guardian is benign and helpful, though somewhat of a nuisance to the hero, since there has never been a shortage of aunts, uncles, friends, neighbors, children, teachers, etc. who want to keep their little hero safe at home.

And thank God for the protectors, because not all threshold guardians are so nice. There are countless minions waiting just outside the door who will do whatever it takes to eliminate the hero and stop the journey before it even gets started. These malignant guardians present a considerable challenge to the newly-appointed hero, but they also serve a fundamental purpose.

> "Many men that stumble at the threshold are well foretold that danger lurks within."
>
> ~William Shakespeare

With the crossing of the threshold, the "ordinary world" is left behind. The hero is about to be "initiated" into the new world by countless trials, attacks, and obstacles. These dangerous threshold guardians are the hero's first test in the new world. But they are also a wake-up call. They show the hero just what this strange new world is all about, and they prepare him for what lies ahead. They are an essential part of the hero's training, because as bad as they may seem now, there are much, much worse things out there. The hero will find out about *that* soon enough.

Application to Christian Life

Are there "protective" threshold guardians in the life of a Christian? Absolutely, and yes, they can certainly hinder the hero's progress on their faith journey. An example is the secular teacher who tries to talk her star pupil out of attending the seminary. She doesn't "get" what his calling, his quest, is all about. She sees that he could become *anything*; an engineer, a doctor, a lawyer! She sees his choice as a tragic waste of brains and talent. She cares about her student, and in her mind she is trying to prevent him from making a terrible mistake. She thinks she knows what's best for him.

> *"[Children] have been loaned to us temporarily for the purpose of loving them and instilling a foundation of values on which their future lives will be built."*
>
> *~James Dobson*

None of us are immune from becoming a protective threshold guardian. It is our love for the person involved that causes us to want to choose the "easy" path for them. It is time yet again to turn to our only tried-and-true source of wisdom and guidance; the Word of God. Listen to the person. Hear what their plans are, and why they think God is leading them in this direction. Pray for them, and consult your Bible. Just as with a crossroads decision, if you can't find a reason that their choice isn't God-pleasing, then give them your blessing and send them on their way. Assure them that God is always with them, and that you will be there for them, too.

You've done that. Good. So why is your heart suddenly gripped by fear as you watch them take their first steps on a journey that will lead them to only God knows where? *Because you know what's out there.* There is another kind of threshold guardian, prowling like a lion, waiting for a chance to pounce and devour. And it is at this moment – having just left the safety of home and the ordinary world – that your loved one is at their most vulnerable. They have not been tried or tested yet, and they are about to face the full fury of the Evil One's assault. What can you do?

> *"Another possible source of guidance for teenagers is television, but television's message has always been that the need for truth, wisdom and world peace pales by comparison with the need for a toothpaste that offers whiter teeth and fresher breath."*
>
> ~Dave Barry

43

Pray. Pray hard. Ask God to give them strength, courage, and a discerning heart. Remember, *they must go through this ordeal in order for God to equip them for what's ahead!* Commit their path to the Lord and trust in Him to watch over them. Let them know that you are there for them if they need you, but this is *their* journey, not yours. They can't become the hero that God is shaping them into without undergoing the trials and obstacles in the dangerous new world.

Danger!

Be careful! Not *every* person who tries to stop you from doing something that popped into your head is a "protective threshold guardian"! Don't read this and suddenly take a patronizing, condescending attitude toward every parent, friend, and advisor who tries to help you. I said that *God* knows better than they do, but a lot of the time *you* still don't! So listen carefully to their advice, and then *you* also need to spend some time in prayer and meditating on Scripture before

> "A true friend never gets in your way unless you happen to be going down."
>
> ~Arnold Glasow

you start breaking the fourth commandment all over the place! Got that?!

There *really is* some terribly evil stuff out there, and your parents and teachers *really do* know more than you about what it is and how to deal with it. So let them help you! Don't let your pride stop you from calling out for help; you have God and probably a whole bunch of people who are waiting to come to your aid. Failure is also part of the training process for God's warriors, but it won't do you any good if you don't survive whatever it is you failed!

8. At some point, there is a "refusal of the call"

Every hero has their breaking point. At some point along every journey, there comes a time when the hero is ready to simply pack it up and head home. It's too much, I quit; someone else can deal with this now. Sometimes the hero tries to back out of the quest right at the start (Moses, Gideon, Jonah?). Even so, there often comes a time later on in the quest that the hero decides he should have taken a right instead of a left at that last crossroads decision.

> *"Our greatest weakness lies in giving up. The most certain way to succeed is always to try just one more time."*
>
> ~*Thomas Edison*

We can hardly blame the heroes when we see what they've been going through. It would be easy to just go back home to the "ordinary world", right? Ha, you're too smart for a trick question like that. No, you just realized exactly what the hero (thankfully) realizes: There is no going back. I'm not the same person anymore. The world has changed, too. If I don't finish this journey, who will? Besides, where will I run to?

And that's exactly what we love about our heroes, and that's one of their defining characteristics. They may give up from time to time, but they never *really* give up. They get frustrated and discouraged. Who doesn't? But their sense of integrity and perseverance simply won't let them give up, and their compassion won't allow them to let other people down. So they trudge on, or they try again, or they start all over from the beginning, because they believe that this journey *must* go on and it is worth the doing.

Application to Christian Life

Do I even need to write anything here? I will anyway. Sometimes we just want to give up on someone who's heart is hardened against the Gospel. Sometimes we just want to give up on our fellow Christians who can seem so lukewarm and hypocritical. Sometimes we just want to give up on the whole world and let the Devil have his playground back, and we'll just run away to some little Christian commune where we don't have to deal with all the darkness and suffering and hatred.

Sometimes…we just want to give up on the journey altogether.

What do you say to this person who just can't take any more? What if I *don't* really know what they're going through? Start by finding a way that you can help them shoulder whatever burden is weighing them down. No hero was ever able to do it all on their own – you'll find out about that in the next two sections. So why do Christians think they're any different? As you look for ways to help this person, pray continually for them. Find ways to strengthen them through God's Word by gently and lovingly sharing verses that may help with their situation.

And what if that person is me? What do I do when *I* can't take any more? I wouldn't tell this to anyone else, but since it's you, I'll be blunt: You can. God would never give you more than you can handle; this He promises. That's the Devil lying to you, telling you that it's more than you can take. God doesn't make weak heroes.

I know, that's not what you want to hear. That's okay, I've got more. Find help. First call out to God and take hold of His Word and cling to it for dear life, because maybe that's what's on the line right now. Then, talk to your pastor. Talk to a family member, a Godly friend, an elder from your church, and tell them what's going on and that you need help. God will provide for even you, the least of these brothers, through His saints.

And lastly...read good Hero's Journey stories! Immerse yourself in quality literature (God's Word first, as always) that teaches, strengthens, edifies, and models heroic behavior! As you read, ask yourself, "What would happen if the hero really *did* give up right now?" You'll soon find that you frequently ask *yourself* the same thing!

9. The hero has a wise and helpful guide

Where would Arthur be without Merlin? Or Luke without Obi-Wan Kenobi? Or Bilbo without Gandalf, or Harry Potter without Dumbledore? Heroes setting out on the quest *need* a wise counselor who will guide and direct them along the first part of their journey. The trials and obstacles of the new world are simply too much for any one person to handle, *especially* some unlikely hero fresh from the village.

Enter "The Wise and Helpful Guide." The guide usually takes the form of a wizard, or a prophet, or some other very old, very wise person. For thousands of years, people have recognized the venerable wisdom of elderly men and women, especially those who have pursued wisdom and scholarship during their lives (like wizards, for

> *"If you young fellows were wise, the devil couldn't do anything to you, but since you aren't wise, you need us who are old."*
>
> ~*Martin Luther*

example; but more on that in chapter 3). The guide cares about the hero personally, and also has a vested interest in the success of their journey. Often, the guide will even accompany the hero on a portion of the quest, and the hero learns a great deal while the guide is so close at hand.

But alas, the hero cannot fully develop his skills and abilities if the guide is always right there to get him out of trouble. Sooner or later, the hero will experience the loss of his beloved guide, sometimes even to death. This is a terrible setback for the hero. If someone as powerful and wise as *him* couldn't even make it through to the end, how will *I* ever? Frequently, this is a point where we might witness a "refusal of the call." But the guide was wise enough to understand that sooner or later the hero would need to stand on his own two feet, and that's just what has to happen now.

So the quest goes on, without the guide. But the hero soon realizes that the guide is never really gone. All the kind words, all the helpful advice, the courageous spirit, the indomitable will; all them live on inside the hero, and the guide continues his vital work long after his departure. And it is not uncommon for the guide to even return later (if not physically, in some form or another), after the hero has had a chance to prove to himself that he can carry on alone.

Application to Christian Life

So which are you, the guide or the "guided"? Either way, you must understand that this is a critically important aspect of the hero's journey, and that means that you have a tremendous amount of responsibility on your shoulders; either to *be* the right kind of guide, or to *find* the right kind of guide.

There can be no higher calling than that of the Christian guide. If you have earned the level of respect where people willingly come to you for counsel and direction on the Christian journey, then you are in a unique class of faith warriors. "Well…" you say, "…maybe they just don't really know me all that well." Okay, we can work with that.

Being a guide for other Christians *is* a huge responsibility, but it doesn't have to be tremendously difficult. You don't even have to have all the answers. Here's the secret: God has already given us a perfect guide for life in which He reveals His will for us in every situation. To be a good guide, all you have to do for the heroes under your wing is point

> *"O that the Lord would guide my ways to keep His statutes still! O that my God would grant me grace to know and do His will!"*
>
> *~Isaac Watts*

them to God, and point them to His Word. It's that simple. To be a *great* guide, you will need to be spending a considerable amount of time in God's Word yourself, so that you can point the heroes a little more specifically. Don't try to impress anyone with your own smarts; let God speak for Himself. "Trust in the Lord with all your heart and lean not on your own understanding" (Prov. 3:5).

Now, for the rest of you heroes who are in the market for a guide, you know what to be looking for. Who can you go to who exhibits a Godly life? Find someone who has deep roots in the faith, someone who has already walked the path of life with God, and develop a relationship with them. If you already have someone like that in your life, then you are truly blessed! Thank God for giving you such a wise parent, spouse, friend, teacher, pastor, neighbor, grandpa, etc. and keep them up to date on how your journey is going.

Danger!

Guides are absolutely *essential*! That is why it worries me so much that the heroes in many of today's stories rely on their own guides so *little*! Most of the heroes in the stories are young; teenagers or younger. And yet they try to tackle all the problems in their lives (and they're usually really *big* problems!) with little or no help from all of the wise, capable adults in their lives. What a sad, dangerous thing to be showing our children!

Naturally, young people love reading books where the kid heroes solve all the problems while the ignorant, out-of-touch, doofus adults stand by, oblivious to what's going on. This is not only unrealistic, it's just plain stupid! I mean, these are life-and-death situations that these kids are taking on. Imagine if they failed and someone got killed, maybe one of their friends;

what kind of terrible knowledge would that be for them to deal with the rest of their lives?

Admittedly, quite often adults are a little out-of-touch with what's going in younger people's lives. It isn't *only* the responsibility of the kids to come find us when something is the matter. Adults should try to pay a little more attention to what is happening in their kids' lives. They need to have a relationship with their kids, and their kids need to know that it is safe to come to them with problems (lecturing and punishing can sometimes wait until the immediate crisis is resolved).

If you are a young person, make *sure* that your "guides" are trustworthy, responsible people! If not, find someone who *is* that you can confide in, even if they aren't as "cool" as the other guy. If you are responsible for young people, make *sure* that you know who their guides are. If they aren't coming to you with problems, I can *guarantee* that they're going to someone else, because we both know that *kids have problems.* And you should *both* think about this fact: Teenagers have a tendency to trust the worst possible people when they're in a bind.

> "For the Lord gives wisdom, and from his mouth come knowledge and understanding. He holds victory in store for the upright, he is a shield to those whose walk is blameless."
>
> ~Proverbs 2:6-7

So make sure that the heroes in the stories you're reading have wise and helpful guides who they actually consult regularly. Yes, the hero will need to stand on his own two feet eventually, but you're not *quite there yet*! Trust someone a little older and a little wiser to help you make decisions for now – and remember that smart heroes keep their guides around as long as possible.

10. Hero partners or companions journey along with the hero

Undoubtedly, every hero will be accompanied by other individuals at some point during their quest. There may be times when the hero is utterly alone, and he will often feel this way even when in the company of others due to the weight of the mission he has been given. However, hero partners and companions are essential to the success of any hero; not only because of the physical aid and martial assistance they regularly supply, but also because they provide hope, courage, motivation, support, and friendship when the hero feels he can't go on any longer (see #8).

"Hero partners" are individuals whose goals are aligned with those of the quest. They know what the hero's journey is all about, and wish to ensure its success for their own reasons. Due to the weightiness of the typical hero's journey – which often involves an immense evil that threatens to cause substantial damage to the world – others will inevitably join forces with the hero to conquer the malevolent forces at work.

"Hero companions" are friends, family members, or loved ones of the hero who join the quest merely for the sake of providing love and support. While "hero partners" care first and foremost about the journey and the success of the quest, "hero companions" care primarily about the hero. This distinction causes the two groups to occasionally have very different outlooks on the quest, their relationship to the hero, and their role in the adventure.

> *"A friend loves at all times, and a brother is born for adversity."*
>
> ~*Proverbs 17:17*

Hero partners provide the "practical" support that the hero needs. Since heroes are typically "unlikely," they probably do not have the fighting skills, physical prowess, or worldly wisdom necessary to survive the quest and overcome the challenges along the journey. Partners frequently fill the gaps that the hero's limited experience leave vacant. As the partners travel with the hero and provide whatever aid they can, the hero learns from them. Travelling with these partners and overcoming obstacles alongside them prepares the hero for even greater challenges later, when they will often have to face similar difficulties without the help of their hero partners.

Hero companions provide moral support for the hero. A friendly face goes a long way when times are tough, and heroes often become easily discouraged by the overwhelming odds they are up against, the grave consequences of their own failure, and the irrevocable change and loss they are undergoing personally. It is the job of the hero companions to remind the hero of who he is and what he is fighting for. They hold the hero to his sense of values and "innocence," preventing him from sinking to the same level as the evil which he is fighting. It is the difficult task of a companion to make sure the hero never gives up, even when their heart is breaking for the terrible suffering the hero is undergoing. They are heroes in their own right.

Since hero partners are more interested in the success of the quest than the survival and well-being of the hero, they will often be more willing to see the hero "sacrificed" for the sake of the objective: defeating the powerful evil. It isn't that they don't like or care about the hero, it's simply a matter of "the good of the many outweighs the good of the few." They rarely have any qualms about sacrificing themselves, either, if it increases the likelihood of success (a heroic quality in itself- see #20).

Hero companions, on the other hand, will have serious misgivings about the self-sacrificing nature of the hero. Their hardest task is convincing the hero to keep fighting despite pain and loss, and doing so often requires as great or greater personal sacrifice than on the part of the hero. After all, these are individuals who care deeply about the hero; they are frequently former "protective threshold guardians" who figured that "if you can't beat 'em, join 'em" (and what better way to keep an eye on the one they care about).

Of course, throughout they journey, the roles of those who accompany the hero can change and evolve. Guides sometimes becomes partners or companions, companions can turn into wise and helpful guides, and hero partners frequently take on the role of companions as they develop a relationship with the hero and begin to care about him as a person.

The important thing for hero partners and companions is maintaining a balance between advocating the good of the quest and the good of the hero, and understanding that the two are indelibly related. Their own quest is delicately interwoven with that of the hero, and the temptation is always to usurp the hero's position; especially when they see the inexperience and seeming ineptitude of the "unlikely" hero.

Application to Christian Life

Our walk of faith would be extremely difficult, if not impossible, without the help of others. Apart from "wise and helpful guides," we also need the support of friends and family – especially when confronting some of the darkest trials in the forest of life. God gives us faithful companions to provide aid and succor along our journey, and allowing them to assist us with the challenges we face is essential to becoming the faith hero that God intends us to be.

Sometimes, there are "hero partners" in our life; coworkers, fellow church members, or people in the community who understand our mission to serve others and bring the Light of the Gospel to those around us. They feel a similar calling and know that by working together you can accomplish much more. We can learn a great deal by humbling ourselves and allowing these partners in the faith to assist us with our struggles. God is equipping you to face greater dangers ahead through the wisdom and experience you gain by observing this person in action.

You may find that God has placed you in a position of partnership in someone else's ministry. This doesn't mean that you will be a permanent fixture in their life, or that you should "hijack" their ministry because you feel better equipped to handle it. You have your own journey to think about. But God has placed you with this person to help them and humbly teach them. Be careful not to get a pompous or patronizing attitude. It may be clear to you that the person you are serving lacks Christian maturity,

> *"I expect to pass through life but once. If therefore, there be any kindness I can show, or any good thing I can do to any fellow being, let me do it now, and not defer or neglect it, as I shall not pass this way again."*
>
> *~William Penn*

but God is likely teaching *you* something as well. Focus on providing whatever practical assistance you can; God may have placed you here to teach this person something, but that will most likely happen through your Christ-like example and not tedious sermonizing. When your paths part, continue to pray for this person and let them know that you are willing to help again if they need you.

Faithful "hero companions" are one the greatest blessings God bestows on the life a Christian warrior. These people are the friends who pray for us and support us all the long years of our life. These are the family members who continue to guide and encourage us, even when we have hopelessly lost the path. And of course, this is the spouse whom God has placed us with and who helps us by providing direction, companionship, and assistance along all life's twisting passages.

Sadly, hero companions can be very difficult to find. It is much easier to develop a superficial work relationship or pseudo-friendship than it is to establish a deep, lifelong bond with another person. These kinds of relationships require a tremendous commitment on the part of both people involved, and in today's "busy" mentality, few have the time or energy to actively seek this out – and many consciously avoid it. Yet, when we find ourselves in dire need of moral support or a faithful friend, we wonder why we haven't taken the time to cultivate these relationships.

Chances are, you don't need to look very far to find people in your church, workplace, or community who need a strong hero companion. Be open to God calling you into the life of one or more of these people. Make time to become a part of their life and their journey, and stick with them. They may even be able to provide *you* with some sort of practical help or advice, and the relationship will certainly help you to grow in your walk with the Lord.

11. The hero receives some kind of "talisman" or helpful gift for the journey

A "talisman" is a small physical object that the hero has or receives on their journey that somehow helps them along. It is usually given to them by a guide or companion, and it frequently has been passed down from the hero's father. The talisman will often have magical properties, or it may simply have symbolic significance (i.e. indicating the hero's identity or lineage). Whatever the properties, the talisman generally represents and embodies a quality or ability of the hero.

> *"Courage and perseverance have a magical talisman, before which difficulties disappear and obstacles vanish into air."*
>
> *~John Quincy Adams*

Probably the most common talisman is the "sword." Since swords were expensive, and a well-crafted sword was a valuable treasure, they usually became family heirlooms, being passed down from father to son over generations. Already we can see how a sword would easily become a striking symbol of one's heritage and identity; ownership of a sword often provided proof on one's ancestry or lineage. Combine this with the fact that there is no more useful tool on the quest than a trusty weapon, and it's easy to understand why the sword is the classic talisman. Additionally, swords in legend and fantasy often have magical powers or properties, some of which only manifest themselves for the hero.

King Arthur drew the sword in the stone as a means of proving his identity and kingship. Thereafter, he keeps this sword because it symbolizes his right to rule Britain. Later, when he wields the sword out of a spirit of revenge and hatred, the blade is broken; Arthur has misused the power of the sword as he has abused his own authority, and the sword breaking represents the future demise of his own lordship and government. He later obtains the magical sword "Excalibur," which subsequently is to be the subject of repeated attempts of theft and sabotage. Again we see the representation for usurpation and illegitimate rule through the rightful or false ownership of the sword talisman.

"Talismans" come in many other forms besides swords, from pendants to rings to magical wands. All of them hold special powers or symbolism and embody some attribute of the hero. When the talisman is lost or fails to function, it is usually because there is a breach in the hero's character or a willful failure to use their own abilities in an appropriate fashion.

Just as every hero has the potential for evil, so most talismans can also be used for dark purposes. Besides representing some part of the good nature of the hero, a talisman will often tempt the hero to use his talents and abilities for evil or selfish purposes. The fact that the talisman is a source of *power* makes it inherently dangerous. An unlikely hero is a good choice for a quest because they lack power and authority, and so they are not easily enticed to misuse their abilities. But as the hero's skills, strength, and influence grow, so does the temptation to abandon the quest and seek after their own advancement. The talisman can be both a source and symbol of this process.

Application to Christian Life

We have been given many gifts to use on our Christian journey. Our intelligence, athleticism, charisma, wisdom, and wealth are all gifts from God, given to us with the intention that we use them to benefit ourselves and others during our journey. But there is always the temptation to use these gifts and abilities for mere pleasure or profit. We ought to see strength, wealth, and power as gifts from God to use for the protection of the weak and innocent, and for the advancement of His kingdom. But instead, we are tempted to use all of our other abilities and God-given gifts for the acquisition of these three elements – which we use in turn to serve only ourselves and the Devil (see #16).

That is why it is so important that we ask God for *only enough* strength, wealth, or power to accomplish the task that He has given us. Why would we want any more? Because we have other selfish reasons in mind. And yet we should know that any excess of these life-giving gifts would be a toxin to our faith and health, corrupting our true self in Christ and diverting our quest completely.

How do we make sure that we will use our gifts in a wise and God-pleasing manner? As always, we turn to His Word for guidance and spiritual strength. Pray, asking God to protect you from your own evil desires. *Flee* from temptation instead of flirting with it. If you know that too much power will tempt you to corruption, then avoid opportunities to advance your position. Ask your guides, partners, and companions to help you use your gifts for God and others, and have them hold you accountable when you fail to do so.

> *"We have different gifts, according to the grace given us. If a man's gift is prophesying, let him use it in proportion to his faith. If it is serving, let him serve, if it is teaching, let him teach; if it is encouraging, let him encourage; if it is contributing to the needs of others, let him give generously; if it is leadership, let him govern diligently; if it is showing mercy, let him do it cheerfully."*
>
> *~Romans 12:6-8*

Most importantly, we must utilize our most valuable and most powerful gift as often as possible. We have been given a "sword" to use and safeguard along our journey, and there is no more crucial element to our success. The Sword of the Spirit, the Word of God, has been passed from the Father to His sons and daughters that they may carry it with them on their quest and always be reminded of their true identity as His children. We have received this precious gift from our Heavenly Father and, in turn, from our earthly fathers, in order that we may continue to fight for what is good, noble, and pure. It is a tool for our own survival and a weapon for service to others. It is the means of faith in our lives; and while we can willingly cast it away, nothing can ever break it or dull it or steal it away from us. Thanks be to God for arming us with such a splendid and priceless heirloom!

Danger!

Any time an object has "magical" or "mystical" powers, we ought to be at least somewhat on guard until we've discerned the context of the element. "Talismans" serve as an excellent allegory for how a person can use their gifts for good or evil, and generally show the consequences for doing either. Most of the time, any magical powers or properties will simply serve to enhance this literary and spiritual application. But occasionally, there are items included that could be dangerous to young, impressionable Christians.

The main question to ask is this: Does this element point me or my child to a real-world form of witchcraft? Does this promote or encourage exploration of Voodoo, Shamanism, Nature Worship, Wicca, or Eastern Mysticism? Or is the "magic" used here distinctly removed from any real spiritual application? If a character has a magic necklace that allows them to breath underwater, it's probably pretty harmless. But if the character's talisman is a small straw doll that a witch doctor in Haiti soaked in human blood and consecrated to an evil spirit, I'd think twice before letting my child read the rest of the story. Here I will refer readers to the discussion of magic in item #3 ("Danger!") section of this chapter, and also to chapter two, where the use of magic in fantasy literature is more fully explored.

12. The hero will eventually "embark upon the quest" with full knowledge of the road ahead

If you remember from #4 (the "Call to Adventure"), the hero rarely knows what he or she is getting into when first setting off from home. Upon entering the new world, all of their expectations and presuppositions about what the adventure is going to be like come crashing down on their heads. Coming to understand just what they are involved in is a long and brutal process. They are beset by ruthless enemies and lured by their own weaknesses to turn back. As they spiral further down along their journey, they slowly procure more information and a greater understanding of just how much they may have to sacrifice in order for the quest to succeed.

Eventually, there is a moment when the hero comes to the realization that if they are going to proceed, it's going to have to be for the long haul. Maybe they *don't* know exactly all the grisly details of the road ahead (they almost certainly don't), but they *do* understand that this is something much bigger than they realized and now they need to decide if they still want to go through with this journey. It's the "Call to Adventure" and "Refusal of the Call" all over again, only on a bigger scale – and this time, it's for keeps.

> *"Here is the world. Beautiful and terrible things will happen. Don't be afraid."*
>
> *~Frederick Buechner*

Just because the hero goes on from here doesn't mean that they won't ever want to turn back again (see#16). But now that they understand the enormity of their own situation and the consequences of continuing, the hero can take a greater level of personal responsibility for whatever destiny lies in wait. Up until now, the hero has been allowed to be a "victim" of sorts – "I didn't ask for this," "I don't deserve this," "Why is this happening to me?" sort of thing. Now they will be leaving that excuse behind.

Of course, a greater level of responsibility on the hero's part also means a higher level of ownership in the quest and an increased commitment to its success. The journey finally becomes "my journey" or "my quest" (which can have its own temptations…), so the hero puts even more energy and personal involvement into the mission. Ironically, it is when the hero first realizes the tremendous amount of sacrifice that may be demanded from him that he first begins to develop a willingness to give up everything for the sake of the quest.

Application to Christian Life

Sometimes our walk with God forces us to make difficult choices. You may have thought from time to time, "If I knew that being a disciple of Christ was going to mean *this*…". When we first began this journey, we really didn't know what we were getting into. In fact, it wasn't even *our* decision to start this journey; God reached out to us through the means of grace, just as the heroes of our stories are drawn into their adventures through no choice of their own. It starts at baptism, or upon the hearing the Word of God, where the Holy Spirit kindles the fire of faith in our hearts and says, "Now out the door with you; you've got a long journey ahead!" And before we knew what was happening, we were going through high school and college, moving into the work force and finding a vocation that matches our Christian calling.

So no, when the "Call to Adventure" came, you could never have known just what would be in store for you down the road. Now you find yourself understanding a little more of what Christian discipleship means and seeing a bit more of the big picture, and you've had a taste of how hard things might be in the future if you insist on pursuing the quest God has given you. Will you "embark upon the quest," knowing full well what sacrifices God may ask you to make in His name? Or will you instead take the wide, easy road of the world, at best living a lukewarm sort of Christianity that does little to fight the darkness closing in all around us? It is a choice that all heroes must make each day as they set out once more.

> *"Expecting the world to treat you fairly because you are good is like expecting the bull not to charge because you are a vegetarian."*
>
> ~Dennis Wholey

13. The hero undergoes a period of "seemingly aimless roaming"

Things were moving along so well, and then all of a sudden...

Lost. Hopelessly wandering, searching for the path, walking and walking while the shadows lengthen all around. Every hero ends up here at some point. It is the most dismal part of the whole wretched adventure. It is a period of simply going around in circles.

Sometimes the hero is literally stuck in a maze or labyrinth, with no directions – monsters lurking around every corner and deadly traps every step of the way. This "seemingly aimless roaming" can also take place in a dark forest, a network of caves or tunnels, a festering swamp, or any manner of wilderness terrain. In some fantasy or science fiction stories, it could even happen in a crowded city, an enormous research facility, or a massive intergalactic battle station.

The worst part of the "seemingly aimless roaming" is that the hero *feels* like he's getting nowhere. All the time, the clock is ticking and the hero and his companions feel the increasing urgency of defeating the powerful evil before it's too late; but here they are, hopelessly lost or stuck inside the labyrinth. Morale hits an all-time low as the members of the adventure begin to despair. Every step forward seems to take them two steps back, and after hours, days, or even weeks of travelling, they seem to be no closer to the end than when they started.

And to top it all off, they are constantly fighting off terrifying enemies and avoiding lethal traps.

But the hero *is* making progress, although he cannot see it now; perhaps not in a sense of physical proximity to his evil adversary, but rather on the journey as a whole. You see, the journey is more than just travelling from point A to point

> *"Smooth seas do not make skillful sailors."*
>
> ~*African Proverb*

B. Once the hero reaches the end of the road, there will be an awful objective yet to fulfill. The journey is about the hero changing, becoming better and smarter and stronger, so that he can defeat whatever is waiting for him at the end. The hero probably wishes that he could just skip all this "aimless wandering about" and arrive at his destination, but that that would be tragically fruitless.

As the hero wanders around, fighting monsters and using his wit and cunning to avoid deadly snares, he is gaining the skills, strength, and courage that he will need later on. He's learning how defend himself from a wide array of dangerous enemies. He's learning how to think quickly in life-and-death situations. He's learning how to keep moving forward even when things look hopeless. This period of "seemingly aimless roaming" is *absolutely critical* to his success on the quest as a whole. Even if he *could* skip through it all and face the powerful evil that threatens his world, it would only end in utter defeat and failure, because he hasn't been trained and equipped properly.

The seemingly aimless roaming is the most important part of the trials and obstacles that the hero faces in the new world. It is what makes weak, naïve, cowardly individuals into strong, savvy, courageous heroes. This "trial by fire" refines and purifies the heroic traits and characteristics that already existed within the hero's personality.

Application to Christian Life

In every stage of a Christian's life, it is easy to believe that "now I've really got this whole faith thing figured out." We think that we've finally discovered what it means to have a close walk with the Lord and a deep understanding of His will and His ways. And then, of course, five years down the road, we look back on that former self and realize how much we have grown and changed since then.

While this can be a bit depressing – like constantly reaching the top of the mountain just to realize that another valley lies beyond – it should also be encouraging. If we looked at our faith of five or ten years ago and did *not* see any significant change or growth, it would tell us that we are spiritually stagnant; trapped in one of life's many bogs or mires and waiting either to sink or be pulled out. If anything, it should serve to keep us humble, never believing that we have all the answers (because we obviously never will).

Other times, it may feel like we aren't making any progress at all. Sometimes the hero thinks he's almost to the end of the maze, only to realize he's come right back to the beginning; other times the hero feels like he hasn't gotten anywhere at all, and then discovers that the exit was just around the next corner. Our constant sins and failures, the relentless attacks by the Devil, and the crushing wickedness of the world around us sometimes make us feel like we haven't gained an inch of ground since our baptism.

Thank God for allowing us to wallow in the midst of trials! We *are* being equipped for the fight ahead, in ways that we can never imagine now. God is the only one who knows the tribulations and opportunities that the future holds for us. Make the most of this "seemingly aimless roaming" by gaining strength and wisdom from the wearisome burdens you are currently bearing. Ask God to help you see His plan for your life and for the courage to continue faithfully on even when you can't see it.

You journey is a bound to be a perpetual state of arming and preparing for what's ahead. Don't worry about the end of the journey or the dragons that lie in wait; focus on the lesson God has given you *today* and you will be ready for anything. Consult your "training manual" (Bible) daily to help you understand and apply the life lessons that God is teaching you. Remember, the Word of God is your sure and trusty Sword against the Devil's attacks; keep it close and keep it sharp!

14. The hero must descend into "the Underworld," a place of great evil or danger

A cherished companion has been taken captive by the forces of darkness, and the hero must infiltrate their gloomy stronghold to free the prisoner. Or the hero and his entourage have been captured by the enemy, and must now orchestrate a daring escape. Or the hero assaults the sinister foe's bastion in order to procure secret information about how to defeat them forever.

At last, one way or another, the hero must finally plumb the depths of evil in a heroic attempt to enter the lion's den. It is a desperate venture, but the hero and his companions know that the only glimmer of hope for success rests with this expedition. They understand full well that there is a good chance that some or all of them may never return. But what choice do they have?

> *"If you're going through hell, keep going."*
>
> ~Winston Churchill

Sometimes the hero must *literally* go into the underworld, like Aeneas or Hercules, entering hell itself and confronting the dangers and terrors there. Usually, the "underworld" is represented by the heart of all evil and darkness – the home and stronghold of the powerful evil that threatens the hero's world. The audacity of such an action is often the only reason it can even hope to succeed; the enemy would never suspect that anyone would dare to assault him in his own fortress. The heroes will need stealth and the element of surprise to avoid instant annihilation.

Obviously, the hero has changed a great deal since the initial "Call to Adventure" to even dare such a feat. His sense of duty and obligation to the quest compels him forward, even if he does not expect to come back alive. Often, he believes himself fully prepared and equipped for this final leg of the quest, although he realizes that any level of preparation may not be adequate to help him survive danger of this magnitude.

What the hero will soon realize is that he still has *much* to learn, and this near-suicidal infiltration is only another part of his training. He cannot yet fully understand or appreciate the awful power of his nemesis, but he will soon get his first glimpse...

Application to Christian Life

American revolutionary Thomas Paine penned the words, "These are the times that try men's souls." At this critical juncture in the war, soldiers all around him were considering abandoning the army for lack of pay and food. They were dark times indeed, with the fate of the war, the nation, and the future of freedom hanging on the brink of collapse. So Paine asked his fellow revolutionaries to examine their hearts and find the courage to press on, into the dark recesses of "the unknown."

As mentioned at the beginning of this chapter, there *will* be dark times in the life of every Christian. Some of them may be shared by the larger Christian community – the oppression of the Church, the growth of secular humanism and New Age religions, and the consequences of a world that embraces sinful lifestyles and deceptive philosophies – but many times they will be individual difficulties and tribulations.

> *"Troubles are often the tools by which God fashions us for better things."*
>
> ~Henry Ward Beecher

Whether it is a global crisis or a personal challenge, these "dark times" represent a considerable challenge in our faith journey. Despite all of the training that God has put us through up to this point, we find it difficult to move forward knowing the sacrifices that may be required of us. We often look for "an easier way," one that would allow us to circumvent some of the pain and hardship but may not be quite as God-pleasing. We are tempted to make concessions and compromise our beliefs in order to ensure a smother road ahead (see #16).

What would happen to the world if the heroes of our stories chose to avoid the "underworld" altogether? What if they elected to save their own skins rather than boldly confronting the dangers that lie before them? We know perfectly well that in the end, this would only make things worse; not only for the rest of the world, but even for the hero himself. To alter course and allow the evil to grow will only delay the present suffering and exchange it for a worse fate later on. Sometimes the hero must "strike while the iron is hot" to avoid losing the opportunity to deal evil a crushing blow, regardless of what it means for his personal comfort and safety.

Sometimes entering the "underworld" is simply unavoidable, like when the hero has been captured by the dark forces and must now plot an escape. At times, we can't avoid facing the dark, narrow road that lies before us even if we want to. It becomes a question of *how* we are going to walk that path. It is a choice between courage and cowardice, steadfastness or wavering, hope or despair. The death of a loved one puts us on the brink of a vortex of anger, resentment, and hostility toward God. Our faith is tested like never before, to the point of breaking completely. But God has promised that He will never allow us to be tested beyond what we can bear. It is our own choice whether we allow the last chords of our faith to snap and sever our relationship with God or fight, hold fast, and allow the wound to heal in such a way as to make us stronger than ever before.

Like the hero in the story, we often think that our training is sufficient for even the most terrifying dungeon of the enemy. And like him, we find ourselves confronted with challenges more difficult than we ever thought possible. Just as the hero finds the strength to go forward into the "underworld," so will we find the strength to face whatever Satan throws our way in life; and by relying on God's grace, we will eventually emerge victorious.

Danger!

Some heroes face a different kind of underworld. Instead of an actual, physical location with dangers and enemies all around, they will descend into the "underworld" of themselves. There is nothing inherently *wrong* with this kind of "descent into the underworld"; after all, the fact that the evil the hero is fighting against is also a part of himself that must be overcome is an important theme in this type of story. But there are some pitfalls to be avoided in how this particular flavor of "underworld" is handled.

Is it clear that what the hero is doing is *wrong*? Are there consequences for this "descent into darkness," or is it simply another means of fighting against an oppressive foe? Remember that the hero must retain a part of his innocence in order to set himself apart from the evil that he is fighting. If the story is teaching that it's okay to engage in all sorts of wicked and illicit behavior, so long as it is directed at the "bad guys," then it's promoting one of the most dangerous lies in our society today. Even *if* this was okay (and it certainly isn't), it's only one step further to hurting "innocent" people for the sake of the "greater good."

Even if the hero is the only one affected by his own descent, the danger of the situation must be clearly evident. It's easy to think of this kind of descent as just another "sacrifice" for the sake of others. But there are some things that should never be sacrificed, no matter what you think the outcome will be. Giving up your faith or compromising your beliefs for the sake of achieving some goal will only lead to destruction. God doesn't ask us to cleverly navigate the morality maze by justifying our own actions with excuses and technicalities; He asks us to do His will and trust in Him to make it end up alright.

If you find that your hero is descending into a "personal underworld" involving their morals, beliefs, or code of ethics, watch carefully for how the author handles this situation. It is likely that they are subtly teaching something about their own beliefs, which can be good or bad. Remember that when you make a choice to willingly descend into darkness, for whatever reasons you tell yourself, you really might not make it out again.

15. The first encounter with the "dark side" proves too difficult for the hero's current abilities

This is it; the showdown. At last there shall be a conclusion. The hero has valiantly fought through countless enemies and survived unimaginable horrors to come face to face with his archenemy. The two of them square off, swords clash, and then…!

Defeat. Failure. Utter ignominy. In short, the hero gets his butt kicked, and hard. He barely escapes with his life, and it's hard to believe he even managed that much. But the worst part is, now everything the hero thought he knew is thrown into shadow and doubt.

He's just too strong. That's the one thought that the hero is left with; that there's no way to ever beat this...thing. How could I endure so much and come this far only to fail now? I never imagined that the enemy was *this* powerful!

This is a trying time for the hero. He has passed so many obstacles, gained so much power, and was just *certain* that there would finally be an end to this whole maddening journey. And now, it seems, we're back to square one, with no idea how we're going to win. Maybe I should just give it up...

"No!" we're thinking. "You can't give up now! There *must* be a way!" Of course, we're right. This first encounter has served a purpose – to show the hero what he's up against. If he can get over the despair that he's facing right now, *next* time he'll be ready. Haven't we learned by now that *everything* the hero experiences is part of his training and equipping for future battles? It shouldn't come as a surprise that inglorious defeat is no exception.

> *"Being defeated is often a temporary condition. Giving up is what makes it permanent."*
>
> *~Marilyn vos Savant*

So the hero picks up the pieces and moves forward in a different direction. Instead of going straight back to face the powerful evil again, he focuses on finding a weakness, or a secret weapon, or some hidden method of finally defeating this villain and putting an end to his wicked ways...

Application to Christian Life

Man, did I ever blow it this time! I thought I was stronger than that... I can't believe how I utterly failed, again, when faced with temptation that I *should* be able to resist. Where is my faith? How can I ever face my friends, my family, my God? Why do I even keep trying when I all I do is fail?

Christians can be a headstrong bunch. We think we're so tough, we think our faith is bulletproof, we think we can handle anything. Our own cockiness just goes to show how spiritually immature we are. A seasoned veteran of the faith knows his own weakness. He knows that his own strength is no match for that of his sinful nature, and that Satan and the world are adversaries not to be taken lightly.

"But wait," you say, "I thought you said that God would never allow me to be tempted beyond what I can bear?" That's true, He doesn't. And that's the really depressing part.

We continually *choose* evil. We constantly *choose* sin and rebellion to God. He always provides a way out of temptation, and we pretend we don't see the open door because we're having too much fun. We so often have a choice between facing temptation with our own power or turning to God's Word for strength. You know the results of both choices as well as I do.

It's true; we're no match for the Devil. He's just too powerful. After all, even if I *could* make all the right choices and avoid temptation my whole life (insert laugh here), there is still the fact that I was conceived and born sinful. I'm defective from the start because of the curse my ancestors brought upon me. The powerful evil is too strong for me in so many ways.

> *"Be self-controlled and alert. Your enemy the devil prowls around like a roaring lion looking for someone to devour. Resist him, standing firm in the faith."*
>
> *~1 Peter 5:8-9*

That's why the *real* Hero's Journey, the *original* Hero's Journey, is so important. We *need* Jesus Christ and His victory over sin, death, and the Devil. He is the *only* One who could go toe-to-toe against all the powers of darkness, fight relentlessly, and finally sacrifice Himself to defeat them. And it is His resurrection that gives me the power to come before God, despite my failures, and receive forgiveness and the strength to fight again.

So fight your hardest, but let your failures be a part of your training. Learn from your mistakes; memorize the enemy's tactics. Arm yourself with the weapons and armor found in God's Word, and then go back onto the battlefield to confront the evil once more. Don't boast, unless it is to boast in your weakness and tell everyone how God's Son defeated the Devil for *you*. In doing so, you will strike a blow to the enemy that will leave him reeling.

16. The hero will be tempted or seduced to join the "dark side"

After the hero's terrible defeat at the hands of the powerful evil entity, he is usually at one of his weakest, most vulnerable states. This is the perfect time for his enemy to coerce, bribe, or tempt him to join forces. The hero has lost all hope and courage, and many times he has survived only because his adversary willed it so, for the sole purpose of persuading him to change sides. Joining the forces of evil may be the only way to escape destruction...

Villains aren't stupid. The evil foe has watched the hero along his journey, tracking his progress and noting his success. This "hero" *could* be a powerful ally. But can he be coerced into joining with us? One method, as mentioned above, is to make him believe that he has no other choice. What could be gained by death? Why not join "the winning team," especially since they are going to win whether you live or die? The hero might even tell himself that he'll join, and then try to overthrow the evil regime from within.

Perhaps the hero's love for his allies, his loved ones, or his guide could be exploited. After all, it would be easier for him to do evil if he *thought* that he was doing it in order to save someone else. Or maybe the hero has a weakness for power, or wealth, or knowledge that can be used to seduce him into our ranks? Maybe we can even lure him in with the promise of some kind of "bargain." We'll make him believe that we'll show mercy or leniency toward certain people if he'll only cooperate with us. Perhaps he'll be more likely to help us if he is shielded from *seeing* anyone actually being harmed.

Whatever happens, the enemy will be certain to present his offer as simply "another path." He's not asking the hero to *abandon* the quest, just to take a sort of detour, or alter the destination. In his weakened state, the hero will be very susceptible to any suggestions of change, since he was already weary of the adventure some time ago. And quite often, the enemy will approach the hero as someone who "only wants to help" him; a friend, who is giving him an opportunity for something better. The enemy shows the hero all the faults of his comrades, and points out the thanklessness of those that the hero is fighting on behalf of.

Now the struggle for the hero is to once more put "self" behind and place the needs of others first. That won't be easy; *my* needs are clear, immediate, and desperate – *their* needs are distant and removed from all of this. Besides, why is that *my* problem? Shouldn't they be able to take care of themselves? Of course, they can't, and the hero knows this. He has been given the skills, the knowledge, the opportunity, and the will to fight this evil, and if he doesn't follow through, the others will perish. Now it's time to make a choice...

The hero might refuse the offer, embracing his own destruction and the end of the journey. But the journey doesn't end; there is a miraculous escape or an unexpected rescue that will no doubt inflame the wrath of the enemy like never before. Or perhaps the enemy keeps the hero alive to continue the process of seduction, or to follow him back home to find more innocent victims, or for some other nefarious reason. However it happens, the hero escapes after staying true to the quest and his determination to fight the evil is fortified even more than before.

If the hero succumbs to the threat of destruction, or to the enticement of power, riches, mercy, or whatever is presented to him, he soon finds out that the bargain wasn't worth it. He regrets his decision, and is once more steeled in his resolve to destroy the powerful evil once and for all. At some point, he may have to "atone" for his traitorous defection, and he now understands that part of the enemy's power *is* the ability to tempt or seduce others so easily.

Application to Christian Life

The scenario looks something like this: You're in the midst of your own personal "underworld" experience – a period of terrible loss, uncertainty, or other tribulation. You've just undergone a shameful defeat at the hands of Satan, and are doubting your own strength to continue the journey of faith. And then there are those "friends" who keep voicing their opinions about the situation; all for your own good, of course. "You need to worry about yourself right now." "This life is all you have." "It's time to find your *own* path." And these are added to voices already inside your own head. "If God loves me, why is He letting this happen to me?" "Maybe I'd be better off without God." "Is God even really there?"

The Devil has been tempting and seducing heroes of the faith for thousands of years. He knows exactly how, when, and where to hit you for maximum effect. We fall constantly, and each time we sin, the Devil is there ready to question our faith: Do you think God will really forgive *this*? He hits us with the "one-two" punch; first by afflicting us with some calamity, and then throwing the blame on God by saying, "Why would a loving God let this happen to such a faithful person?"

We need to understand that because we are so precious to God, we are also extremely valuable to the Devil. Satan would strike back at God by afflicting and abducting His children. If God really *didn't* care about us, then Satan wouldn't have any reason to harm us. But the fact is, we are the only part of this world that matters to God, so the Prince of this world will focus the battle on *us*.

When Satan engages his "temptation or seduction" tactics against me, he isn't just after *me*, either. Just like in the Hero's Journey story, Satan knows that you are a valuable weapon in his hands. He is aware of what an awful impact it would have on the faith community, if only he can entice away a long-time Christian warrior like you. The terrible notion would spread through the murmuring saints; "I never would have believed it possible! If *his* faith can be broken..." Satan knows that by turning you against God, you can become his "missionary" among all those who are weak or struggling in their own faith journeys.

If faithful Job can be brought to his breaking point by the Devil's lies, then we should certainly understand that he is a threat to us as well. Like Job, we need to seek the counsel of Godly friends and companions. We need to turn to God and His Word at this critical time, when our anger and disgust with Him makes that the last thing we want to do. And like Job, we will find that when the storm has passed, our faith is even stronger than before it was tested. Like the hero in the story, we will know all the better the awful power of the enemy and find a new will and determination to go out and fight him with all our might.

> *"Blessed is the man who perseveres under trial, because when he has stood the test, he will receive the crown of life that God has promised to those who love him."*
>
> *~James 1:12*

85

17. The hero has a "tragic flaw" that continually puts him in danger

The hardest battle the hero will fight along the journey will be against *himself.*

That's right. As if it weren't bad enough that he's been ripped from the world he knows and loves, has to face horrible monsters and enemies all along the way, and constantly escape from life-threatening situations. Now we find that his own worst enemy is...him.

Heroes come with all manner of flaws to overcome. Sometimes they are purely physical disadvantages that hinder the hero's abilities. Often the hero is very small or weak, and has trouble climbing, swimming, or lifting things – all actions that heroes routinely need to perform while questing. Or it might be an even more serious condition, like blindness or deafness, which poses a serious threat to the hero's safety and causes him to easily fall into danger, often making it necessary to rely on others. Sometimes this physical "flaw" will even come in the form of asthma, diabetes, or epilepsy, all of which can put the hero's life in jeopardy at very inconvenient times.

More often, however, the flaw is a negative personality trait that the hero *should* be able to control. Even if the hero possesses a physical disability, he will usually have a "character flaw" in addition. This flaw will be the subject of significant focus throughout the journey, with the hero realizing at some point that they will need to confront and overcome it in order to succeed.

> *"In general, pride is at the bottom of all great mistakes."*
>
> *~John Ruskin*

The most common "character flaw" found in classic Hero's Journey stories is that of pride, or "hubris." The hero is stubborn, headstrong, and obstinate. He refuses to take the wise advice of the "guide" or his companions, often because he feels a need to demonstrate his ability to handle things on his own. He foolishly forfeits opportunities for valuable aid or assistance, only to regret the decision in the near future. He takes a dangerous level of ownership and responsibility in the quest, insisting that it's *my* journey. Pride, arrogance, and a persistent refusal to allow others to guide and support him often lead the hero to experience unnecessary pain and heartache.

"Hubris" is a wicked foe. It is especially difficult to defeat because it naturally protects itself against attacks from the hero. That is to say, it is the very "pride" that the hero needs to overcome which will not allow him to humble himself and admit that he's wrong. Something external will need to

> *"Choose rather to be strong of soul than strong of body."*
>
> *~Pythagoras*

provide the catalyst for change, and it will often be a powerfully painful and humiliating experience for the hero. Yet

> *"Temper gets you into trouble. Pride keeps you there."*
>
> *~Anonymous*

again we see how the hero's trials and obstacles in the new world are training and preparing him to face the evil at the end of the journey; physically, mentally, and spiritually.

While an overdeveloped sense of pride is a universal human characteristic and rarely misses an opportunity to manifest itself in any hero, there are plenty of other character flaws as well. Often, the hero lacks confidence, or doesn't believe in his own abilities (ironically, even these characters are not immune to difficulties resulting from a warped sense of pride). Some heroes struggle with excessive anger or hatred that the enemy uses against them. Many heroes tend to be simply "rash," and don't analyze the consequences of their actions until it's too late. Greed, lust, and a hunger for power are other common pitfalls for heroes along their journeys. But generally speaking, each hero will have one vice or flaw that is especially dangerous to them and will struggle with it throughout the journey until they finally overcome it.

> *"'Know thyself?' If I knew myself, I'd run away."*
>
> *~Johann Wolfgang von Goethe*

Character flaws are typically mere signs of incontinence on the part of the hero. The hero isn't willfully performing evil or hurting others, but their own weakness causes them to stumble and hinders their progress. From a literary standpoint, readers have an easier time relating to characters who "mess up," because I know how far from perfection I am. But more importantly, it shows the universal struggle of mankind fighting against our own desires and compulsions, constantly trying to overcome whatever vice we find our hearts in the grip of. It reminds us that in order to be a truly effective hero, we must first conquer ourselves. Perhaps that is the *real* enemy, and the dragon is only secondary...

Application to Christian Life

Even Christians know about flaws. Christians should *especially* understand flaws, because we have the privilege of being reminded of God's law, His perfect will for our lives. This same law has been impressed upon the hearts of all people in our consciences, but Christians ought to have a harder time ignoring it and pretending that our flaws "aren't so bad."

It's hard to fight the Devil *out there*, in the world, if you're losing the battle inside your own heart. Does this mean that I can't effectively show God's light to others unless I stop sinning? Of course not. The power of the Gospel works through its own strength, not ours. And if we're going to wait until we stop sinning completely before entering the battlefield, we're basically forfeiting the war to Satan.

However, our own Christian witness will clearly be less effective when the Devil's will is done in our lives more than God's will. People will hear what we say and look at what we do, and the comparison will be laughable. The hypocrisy will do so much to drive people *away* from the Church that the Devil

> *"The Lord works through deeply flawed people, since He made so few of the other kind."*
>
> *~Timothy B. Tyson*

will be able to sit back and take the day off. Why would anyone want to have anything to do with a bunch of "Christians" who preach love, forgiveness, and compassion but who exhibit hatred and stubbornly hold grudges in their own lives?

Pride is still the most dangerous flaw for Christian life, in many ways. Our sinful pride makes us feel like we're better than our unbelieving neighbors and coworkers; they sense this, and it drives them away. Our arrogant pride makes us refuse to accept help or guidance from family members or pastors who see us mired in sinful behavior. It is our wicked pride that causes us to rebel against God every day, believing that we know better than He does and can handle things on our own.

Apart from our woeful Christian witness, another frightening implication of our flaws is the testament they give to our own spiritual health. Jesus says that anyone can tell the kind of tree by the fruit that it bears. Take a look at your branches; what do you see? Be sure to pull aside the leaves and look carefully, rather than hiding rotten fruit under a thin layer of foliage. Where are your roots? Are they firmly embedded in the rich soil of God's Word? Are you drinking daily of the Living Water as you are reminded of God's promise through your baptism? Are you being nourished with the food that the Lord Himself provides for us through the Sacrament of Holy Communion?

> *"Basically we are all looking for someone who knows who we are and will break it to us gently."*
>
> *~Robert Brault*

We're never going to be perfect; that's why we need Jesus in our lives. His forgiveness allows us to reflect His love to those around us. It empowers our repentance and can effect *real* change in our lives. It gives us the means and the will to overcome those "flaws" that prevent us from boasting in our weaknesses and showing the Light of the world to those who dwell in darkness. And like the heroes in the stories of old, we cannot separate the fight within ourselves from the fight with the dragon, because they are part of the same journey and the same battle.

Satan intends to drive us to despair through our flaws. They are powerful tools that he uses to dissolve our faith and undermine our testimony. But the Devil's plan backfires for God's chosen warriors when instead of being driven to despair, their flaws and failures drive them to the Cross. Our flaws should constantly direct us to God's Word, wherein we see His perfect will for our lives and find the forgiveness of sins that grants newness of life and the strength to keep fighting.

> *"My grace is sufficient for you, for my power is made perfect in weakness."*
>
> ~2 Corinthians 12:9

Danger!

The hero's "tragic flaw" has served as a powerful statement about the universal human condition in countless stories for thousands of years. How is this element reconciled with the notions of secular humanism? After all, they would say, that's just the way the hero is, and there's nothing wrong with that. He's a product of his heredity and environment, and he ought to embrace his personality "quirks" as emblems of his own uniqueness and individuality.

Sadly, the idea of the "tragic flaw" in many modern Hero's Journey stories is being changed to fit the philosophies of today. Instead of the hero overcoming and conquering his flaw, you will now find him (at best) overcoming the powerful evil *in spite of* his flaw. Sometimes, absurdly, stories are constructed in such a way as to make the hero's tragic flaw the *means* by which he is able to defeat the powerful evil!

However it is handled, the moral of this kind of story is this: "Embrace your flaws! They aren't a part of the evil you are fighting; they're a vital part of *who you are!*" This is the kind of thinking that leads Christians to say, "I understand that I can be mean, arrogant, and abrasive toward others. But God made me that way and it's just part of my personality." Are you kidding?! Those traits are not natural; they are a direct result of the curse of sin on this world. God has *nothing* to do with your malice, conceit, or insensitivity. The fruits of the Spirit are love, joy, peace, patience, kindness, goodness, faithfulness, gentleness, and self-control. But out of the heart, which has been corrupted by sin, come all selfish desires, evil thoughts, and wicked counsels.

Only the Father of Lies could convince anyone, especially Christians, that something is *good* when it is obviously and patently evil. Rely on God's Word for the *truth*, and you will know it when you see it in Hero's Journey stories as well.

18. There will be a "death and rebirth" scene

The hero has understood for some time now just how great a sacrifice may be demanded from him in order to accomplish the quest. The time has come for him to lay his life and all that is precious to him on the line for those whom he seeks to save. He must make the ultimate sacrifice in order to finish the task that he has been sent to accomplish.

Sometimes, the hero must literally and physically suffer death in the course of the journey. Whether the hero dies intentionally or suddenly in the course of fighting, his life was given willfully and knowingly for the sake of completing the journey. But what the hero didn't know is that *death will not be the end.*

In some stories, the death scene is purely symbolic. The hero sacrifices *something* that is so dear to him that life as he knows it is over. Or perhaps the hero becomes sick or injured and is in a death-like state. The truth is, the hero has *already* sacrificed his life for the quest by leaving behind home, friends, family, and a bright future. The literal "death and rebirth" scene could just as easily be a metaphor for everything else the hero has given up in order to pursue this adventure.

And then, when all hope is lost, the hero returns. The grave is burst open and the hero is sent back to finish the task that has been appointed to him. The injury or sickness is miraculously healed, and the journey is allowed to continue. The hero shakes off whatever loss was demanded of him and prepares to embark upon the final stretch of the quest.

> *"Our Lord has written the promise of resurrection, not in books alone, but in every leaf of springtime."*
>
> ~*Martin Luther*

It doesn't take long for partners and companions (and enemies) to realize that the hero is somehow different now. He is a new person; stronger, smarter, better than ever before. He radiates a confidence and will to put an end to the powerful evil once and for all. He has powers, either physically or mentally, that he didn't previously possess, and no one can explain where they came from. Perhaps he's had them all along, lying dormant underneath the "unlikely hero" appearance?

The "death and rebirth" scene is an important aspect of life, and that's why it has endured for centuries in this kind of story. Whether it is the hero himself or someone else in the story who experiences it, we are shown and reminded that every end leads to a new beginning and that new life can be found even in the cold clutches of pale death. Hope is reborn, and nothing can stop the hero from faithfully fulfilling his destiny now.

Application to Christian Life

Where does one even *start* with the connections to the life of Christian? Our faith would be meaningless if God's Son had not conquered death, bursting forth in glory on Easter Sunday and giving life and hope to all those who trust His Word of promise. This theme is at the very *core* of the Christian faith, and should be evident each and every day in the life of God's warriors.

Because Jesus Christ suffered on our behalf and defeated sin, death, and hell, we too will one day be reborn. We will cast off this frail flesh and receive a new and glorified body, clothed in the garment of Christ's righteousness. We will not be sent back to fight any longer, but will receive the reward of Jesus' victory; eternal rest and peace in His very presence. We *long* for that day, and it shouldn't be any wonder why we enjoy reading stories that remind us of this magnificent theme.

But that day could be a long way off, and meanwhile we have work to do. Like the hero in the story, we have been given this journey for a reason, and God alone has the power to decide when our task is finished. In the meantime, the "death and rebirth" theme can give us strength to continue our quest until God takes us for our final transformation.

We have already been transformed. You might look at your hands and feet and feel remarkably disappointed, since there is no glorious physical sign of your rebirth emanating from every member. But you experienced a change at your baptism which far surpasses the acquisition of super powers or clairvoyance or mind. You underwent the miracle of faith. You were *dead* in your sins, and you have been made *alive* again. The devil had won, and God smashed into your prison cell, sword flashing heroically, and scattering the demons that guarded your soul He led you to new life. And you have powers now beyond anything that is natural to this world: love, joy, peace, and hope. These weapons will not only guard your own life, but allow you to fight on behalf of all the others who are still chained inside their own prison cells.

"That sounds great," you say, "but I don't think the transformation worked on me. If it had, I wouldn't be doing all the rotten things and saying all the hurtful words that I am." Well, the great part is that God's free forgiveness of sins allows us to undergo the miracle of rebirth and renewal *every day*. We must daily drown the old sinful man in us through repentance and be reborn perfect, holy, and pure.

> *"We died to sin; how can we live in it any longer? Or don't you know that all of us who were baptized into Christ Jesus were baptized into his death? We were therefore buried with him through baptism into death in order that, just as Christ was raised from the dead through the glory of the Father, we too may live a new life."*
>
> *~Romans 6:2-4*

And tomorrow, we'll do it again. In this way, we will constantly be re-equipped to fight the evil in us and around us. God's forgiveness is so powerful that, like the hero, we are a different person afterward.

Danger!

All kinds of varying plot devices are used to effect the "death and rebirth" scene. The important thing to watch for is that the scene is being true to the theme of restoration and renewal. Otherwise, it could simply be a device for incorporating eastern mysticism or ritualistic magic into an otherwise wholesome literary pattern.

Many times, magic is the impetus for the rebirth of the hero. This isn't necessarily bad, and I encourage you to keep reading more about this in chapter two. Magic is often used allegorically, or simply as a means to separate the fantasy world from the real world. That's good, because the danger lies when readers don't differentiate between what is "real" and what is "fantasy." So as long as the character isn't brought back to life by way of a Satanic ritual found in an ancient book of druidic spells (*highly* unlikely for this particular element) or some similarly detailed means of occult magic, the use of magic in the death and rebirth scene probably holds little danger.

Reincarnation scenes are on much shakier ground, however. While such a scene *could* be depicted and explained in a way that would neutralize much of the spiritual danger, they are rarely done so. Reincarnation is a very real part of pagan belief systems, and it teaches gradual salvation through one's own morality. It certainly appeals to people, especially youth, who want to have a sense of control over their own destiny. But it's an illusion, and by the time the truth is unveiled it will be too late. I would approach any story using reincarnation with extreme caution, and would at the very least converse with my child about any book they might be allowed to read that uses this kind of device.

As with any Hero's Journey element, take the time to talk about all of the wonderful connections to their life as a child of God and young faith warrior. Help them to see how these elements demonstrate spiritual truths and can equip us for battling Satan along our own journeys. Make sure they are being fed with the Bread of Life first by keeping them connected with the Word of God, and act as a "wise and helpful guide" as they embark upon new reading adventures.

19. The hero will obtain some "mystical insight" or undergo a "transformation of consciousness"

Ever since first setting out on the quest, and especially since the first disastrous encounter with the dark side, the hero has been searching for a secret. There *must* be a way to defeat the powerful evil the next time I come up against it, but how? The journey has shifted from trying to locate and destroy the enemy to a quest for information; either some secret weakness of the enemy or some hidden weapon or ability that I can use against him. The revelation of this information usually happens in an unexpected way.

At times, the secret of defeating the powerful evil is imparted to the hero through some form of mystical knowledge or insight. Perhaps by and oracle or prophet, or during a journey to the "underworld," or through the reading of an ancient text; somehow or other, the hero suddenly "just knows" what he has to do in order to win. This is Luke

Skywalker's sudden revelation to "use the force" instead of trusting on his targeting computer, or Perseus dancing with the apple nymphs and "absorbing" the knowledge of how to locate the Grey Sisters.

Other times, this secret knowledge comes as a package deal with the total transformation of the hero. This frequently occurs in conjunction with the "death and rebirth" scene, although it can happen completely separately as well. The "transformation of consciousness" is noticeable to those around the hero, either because of "side effects" (i.e. physical change, special powers, etc.) or simply because the hero has a new sense of confidence and authority afterward.

The "mystical insight or transformation of consciousness" is the key to defeating the evil force threatening the hero's world. Often it is something that has been with the hero all along, just out of sight. Many times it means the hero must overcome their own "tragic flaw" or some personal weakness. And sometimes, it will have nothing to do with the hero himself, but instead direct him to a flaw or weakness of the enemy. Whatever it is, the hero is now that much closer to the defeat of evil, and he is ready to encounter the enemy face to face once more.

Application to Christian Life

What could "mystical insight or transformation of consciousness" possibly have to do with being a Christian? It sounds goofy at best, and at worst downright dangerous. But there *are* some secrets and hidden weapons to defeating sin in our lives, after all.

First of all, our *faith* is the most basic, fundamental part of our battle with Satan, the world, and our own sinful nature. And let's be honest, I didn't obtain the "mystical" miracle of faith through my own reason or powers. It was revealed to me by God, through the Holy Spirit who came to me in baptism and through hearing the Word of God. Thanks be to God that he used other Christians in my life and all the circumstances surrounding my birth and upbringing to allow me to encounter His saving Word of life. I have been transformed by the washing and renewal of my heart and mind, and this was all quite outside my own actions or understanding.

This "mystical insight or transformation of consciousness" occurred right along with my "death and rebirth" scene, as often happens in the Hero's Journey pattern. In baptism, I became a new being, and I was given Christ's own victory over the grave to wrap myself in and shield my soul from the Devil's ugly accusations. It was the *only* way he could be defeated.

> *"Do not conform any longer to the pattern of this world, but be transformed by the renewing of your mind."*
>
> *~Romans 12:2*

We encounter other "secrets" along our faith journey as well. Why did I fail when I went up against the forces of evil the last time? All of my training and knowledge and strength weren't enough to beat him; what's up with that, God? It's really no big secret; when we trust in ourselves and our own powers instead of trusting in God and His Word, we're destined to fail.

Or another secret: If God loves me so much, why is He letting all of this happen to me? Well, if a commander cares about his soldiers, he's going to train them as hard as possible. He knows all the deadly weapons and tactics of the enemy, and he wants his men to be prepared for anything. We've already seen how the trials and obstacles the hero encounters in the new world are preparing him for what lies ahead; the threshold guardians, the seeming aimless roaming, even his temptation or seduction by the forces of evil. These experiences are equipping the hero for personal survival and service to those around him. It is no different for a Christian; understanding and believing this fact is part of the "mystical insight" that God provides for us along the way.

"Epiphany" is an important concept in the Christian Church. God unveiled His plan for mankind's salvation in the fullness of time, regardless of human speculation as to how and when it would all take place. I believe this continues on an individual basis for all Christian pilgrims. God reveals His truth to each of us in His own time, choosing to keep some things hidden. Not that His *will* is hidden from us – we can always turn to His Word and discover there exactly what kind of life He would have His children lead. But He leads and guides us through certain experiences in life to help us better understand what his intentions and plans are. Knowing this, we can confidently face every challenge and every new day with the faith that God will provide the means to effectively fight evil and defend ourselves from the attacks of the wicked foe.

20. The hero will have to undergo a physical sacrifice or loss

In the course of the journey, most heroes receive some kind of wound that will remain with them for the rest of their life. They will be left with a physical reminder of all the pain they had to endure throughout the journey. Some permanent scar, disability, or abnormality will leave its mark upon their body, just as the journey has left its mark upon the hero's mind and spirit.

Life will never be the same again. The hero has known this sad fact for quite some time, but the physical loss or sacrifice confirms it. Some wounds cannot be healed, and some hurts can never be undone. But the physical loss is not the greatest sacrifice that has been demanded of the hero, and it only symbolizes something much more important that has been taken from the hero.

As mentioned earlier, the hero has given his life for the sake of the quest. Sometimes this is quite literal, but even if not, the hero has given up everything that he knew and loved about the world he lived in before the journey began. Home, relationships, future plans; all of it has been shattered by the demands of the quest, and the pieces can never be put back together again. The hero is not the same person he once was.

The physical sacrifice or loss embodies the loss of innocence that has taken place, the greatest sacrifice made by the hero. He has witnessed too much pain, seen too many good people die and good things destroyed, learned too many dark secrets, and plunged into the heart of evil on a mission to give life and hope a chance. He saved the world, that is true; but what about *his* world? What about all the dreams he once had? What about the young man who used to be able to look at the world around him and see only what was good and pure and right? All of that has been destroyed for him by the experiences that he has been through. The people he saved will never understand the terrible loss that was demanded for his efforts, and no physical ailment could ever match it.

And yet, in spite of all the terrible things he has witnessed and undergone, the hero knows that the world is a much better place for all of it; not only for everyone else but even for himself and his offspring. The physical loss that he continues to carry with him reminds him of the pain, the effort, and the heartache; but also of the strength, the valor, and the triumph over evil. He keeps these things close to his heart, and shares them with others when he returns home so that

> *"Those things which are precious are saved only by sacrifice."*
>
> *~David Kenyon*

all of it will be preserved and passed on. And one day, the forces of darkness may return; and because he shared his wisdom and experiences with others, someone else will take up the mantle and rise up as a hero.

Application to Christian Life

What is the cost of discipleship? Jesus said that anyone who would come after Him would have to take up their cross and follow Him. He warned us then that there would be a price to pay for doing the Father's will. The early church leaders and martyrs learned this the hard way. Ask any eighth-grader who has stood up for what he believes in a public school, and he can tell you that even here, today, in our "civilized" society, there is a price to pay.

Every Christian sacrifices something. For some, it might mean giving up a shot at fame and fortune in order to pursue a career in professional Church work. Or perhaps it means sacrificing free time to help "neighbors" who God places in your path. Maybe it's a matter of sacrificing treasures for the sake of supporting local and foreign ministry efforts. Some might even sacrifice advancement in a job or their reputation because they are outspoken about their beliefs.

So why do we make these sacrifices? After all, Jesus gave *Himself* as the ultimate once-for-all sacrifice on our behalf, so it isn't like we're earning points with God by giving up our "fun" for Him. We do it because it's important to *us*; because the new creation that is in us drives us to live a life worthy of the great calling we've been given.

Oh, to be sure, our sinful nature still struggles against these impulses, reminding us of how much easier things would be if we'd just realize that it's *my* life and nobody can tell *me* what to do! But that's what makes our small sacrifices so much better. God *doesn't* demand these things; they are our gifts of love to a God who has blessed us with so many good things that we cannot possibly contain them all for ourselves.

In a way, every Christian gives up "the old, comfortable life" upon beginning the faith journey. Like the hero in the story, we leave behind all that the world has to offer and set out on an adventure that promises danger, discomfort, and loss. But when we look back on the alternative, we realize that we've gained so much more than we were ever willing to give up. When one

> *"Greater love has no one than this, that he lay down his life for his friends."*
>
> *~John 15:13*

seeks first the kingdom of God and His righteousness, He really does provide for us richly and abundantly.

21. Against all odds, the hero will finally "slay the dragon"

Any logical, tactical, or analytical perspective would see it as a suicide mission. The chances of success are so infinitely small that they seem non-existent. It is Odysseus challenging over one hundred warriors with only his son and two faithful farmhands to assist him. It is Luke Skywalker attempting to destroy the most heavily fortified battle station the galaxy has ever seen with a puny fighter ship and a proton torpedo. It is the little shepherd boy fearlessly confronting the massive Goliath with only a sling and a few stones.

But the hero has more on his side than meets the eye. Were it not for the journey, he would be instantly crushed. Odysseus has gained the favor of Athena and an incredibly strategic mind throughout his travels. Luke has learned the secrets of "The Force" and has put all fear and doubt behind him. David has trusted in His God to protect him from wild beasts and will not suffer fools who mock the name of the Lord.

The enemy should have known better. By putting the hero through such diabolical trials, he has only helped to create a nemesis of unfathomable strength, spirit, and valor. The hero has come through the worst stretches of the journey already and is now prepared to do whatever it takes to rid the world of this loathsome evil – and willing to accept whatever fate lies before him. A more dangerous foe could never have been constructed by all the craft

> *"Fairy tales are more than true; not because they tell us that dragons exist, but because they tell us that dragons can be beaten."*
>
> *~G.K. Chesterton*

and cunning of the wisest counselors of the Earth. How foolish of the enemy not to have foreseen this outcome; it is an axiom as old as time itself.

The hero can now look back upon all of the trials, all of the obstacles, all of the deadly enemies and traps, all of the pain and suffering and heartache, and he can see how *each and every piece* has been an *essential* part of his development as a hero and a warrior of light. Everything that has occurred so far has led to this moment, and every ounce of knowledge, strength, and will that he possesses, he owes to the journey. He is no longer the weak, frail boy that he was when he first set out on the road, all that time ago. He is a legendary hero of courage, resourcefulness, and fortitude; and he is the only thing standing between the living world and the ravenous, all-consuming evil that is before him.

> *"The greater the obstacle, the more glory in overcoming it."*
>
> ~Moliere

He will not fail. There is no more thought of self; whatever pain, whatever loss, whatever shame he may have to endure for the sake of the world he is protecting, so be it. He will spend himself to purchase peace. There is no going back to the life and world that he once knew, but he can buy years of happiness and hope for those who otherwise might have to follow the path of pain and sacrifice. If he can prevent the next hero from ever needing to *be*, that will be enough to redeem everything he has given up.

The battle may be an epic struggle that rages on for hours, or it may last but a single moment. The hero may have to sacrifice much in the process, perhaps even losing his own life. This final battle is still a part of the journey. Everything the hero has experiences so far *has* been preparing him for this moment, but not *only* for this moment...

> "Here is the test to find whether your mission on earth is finished. If you're alive, it isn't."
>
> ~Richard Bach

This is the one thing that the hero has yet to learn, but will soon find out. The journey will continue even after this. The "dragon" is also a part of himself; sometimes he must vanquish his own weakness in order to destroy the powerful evil, but sometimes they happen together. By undergoing this great quest and facing this monstrous enemy, he has been transformed into a different person; one that will continue to be a hero for years to come.

The hero will help to conquer many dragons for the duration of his lifetime *and beyond*. He will guide and teach others upon returning home, bringing with him a torch of truth that has been kindled by the understanding he

> "There is nothing like returning to a place that remains unchanged to find the ways in which you yourself have altered."
>
> ~Nelson Mandela

gained on this great journey. It will show them the qualities that a hero must possess to overcome evil. It will help them to step wisely on the paths of their own journeys. And it will demonstrate how they are to meet the challenges so that they will be equipped to slay their own dragons when the time comes.

This torch will be passed on to future generations, showing each in turn some helpful truth or illuminating some forgotten part of the human spirit. And if ever a real dragon should rise up in fiery wrath once more, this torch will blaze all the brighter to guide one hero on the path that so many others have walked before. It will burn on, illuminating the gloomy streets of life and clearly marking The Way of the Hero for all those who must travel that dark and difficult road.

Application to Christian Life

Will the Church survive? Sometimes it seems doubtful. The evils of the world press in upon every side, threatening to overtake the dwindling community of the faithful. Animosity toward God and the Church continue to increase, pagan religions find their footholds in every part of our country, and atheism becomes the "faith" of choice for many young adults. Satan is gathering his armies for a massive assault upon the walls of our Mighty Fortress.

Secular humanism kidnaps our children's minds and holds their hearts at a terrible ransom. Those who could have been mighty warriors of the faith are stolen away, quit their training, and pursue a life of emptiness. Our "institutions of learning" feed their minds with lies, convincing them that no one "made" them, no one "redeemed" them, and certainly nothing is going to "preserve" them against the unending tide of deceit and slander that spews from the mouth of the Enemy and washes over them daily. And so the future of the Church is being cut off at the roots.

As if this picture weren't bleak enough already, the precious Church suffers from attacks, sabotage, and neglect even from within its own walls. Many would-be warriors remain safely off the battlefield, for fear of criticism or mockery (as if *not* fighting was the "safe" thing to do!). Others deny that a war even exists at all, claiming that all is well with the world and there is no reason to fight. Some simply feel that it's hopeless anyway, and have too much going on in "life" to worry about the cosmic battle between good and evil, between everlasting life and eternal death for those around them.

The walls of our fortress are weakened by rot as false preachers deny the consequences of sin and fail to point always to the Cross of Christ for salvation. God becomes merely a remedy to social and psychological ills rather than a life-giving Father. Faith becomes a political agenda, just another "means" to achieve a secondary purpose. And so we see the cracks forming in the walls of the Church, "by schisms rent asunder, by heresies distressed."

Things look hopeless. And yet, when the hero in the story relies on everything he has gained from his journey, he finds victory in the face of certain defeat. When success seems like a fleeting illusion, somehow he overcomes the insurmountable task laid before him. So what do we rely on in these dark and troublesome times? In what do we place our hope?

If we have learned anything along our faith journey, it ought to be that the promises of God are sure and certain. God has promised that the Church will stand in the face of all darkness, and that not even the gates of Hell will prevail against it. God's promises

"With might of ours can naught be done, soon were our loss effected; but for us fights the valiant One, Whom God Himself elected. Ask ye, Who is this? Jesus Christ it is, of Sabaoth Lord, and there's none other God; He holds the field forever."

"Though devils all the world should fill, all eager to devour us, we tremble not, we fear no ill; they shall not overpower us. This world's prince may still scowl fierce as he will, he can harm us none. He's judged; the deed is done; one little word can fell him."

~ Martin Luther: A Mighty Fortress is Our God

have the power to defeat giant Philistines, to break the yoke of slavery for His people, and even to destroy the power of sin, death, and the Devil. His promises can and will prevail against all that plagues the Church today.

The Light that has been passed down to us from our fathers will shine all the more brightly as the darkness presses in around us. For thousands of years, this Light has guided heroes of the faith as they stood their ground, put self behind, and boldly sacrificed all for the sake of freeing others from the oppression of Satan's lies. The Light of the World Himself first lit the torches along the path of the hero, clearly marking how His disciples are to walk after Him.

Heroes *will* rise up and fight for as long as God's promises are preached and believed by His people. They will hold the Light high for all to see, even as enemies gather all around and attack them fiercely. These attacks they will gladly endure, because they know that it is the *Light* that matters, not themselves. They carry with them a power that is beyond anything they could ever muster and greater than anything the enemy could ever endure.

When the time is right, God will lead these heroes into the dragon's lair, as onlookers sadly shake their heads. The battle will rage, and the foundations of the Earth and everything that mankind thinks he knows will be shaken. And suddenly, the piercing Light of the Gospel will burst forth from the cave and wash over all the land. The Light will be set upon the highest peak for all to gaze upon and be healed.

It is a time of darkness, true. But it is also a time of *heroes*.

The Ultimate Hero: Jesus Christ

The Bible is the greatest story of all time; all the more so because it is one hundred percent true. What could be more inspiring that the story of God's Son infiltrating a fallen world and conquering the forces of darkness to redeem us? Nothing, of course, and that's why so many "Hero's Journey" stories exist. They are all a testament to the one true Hero and the story of His life, death, and resurrection. Let's go through the Hero's Journey patters one by one and take a closer look:

Genesis chapter 3 gives the details of how our world was plunged into mortal peril. The powerful evil that threatens to consume our world (and our souls) certainly wasn't "unknown" to God. But for the poor wretches dwelling here below, the best we can hope for is a foggy recognition of our true spiritual state. We were *dead* in our sins; dead bodies see nothing, feel nothing, and know nothing. So while we're stumbling around in the dark trying to figure out "the meaning of life" and blissfully unaware of the fiery lake waiting to consume our blackened souls, God sends a Hero our way to save the world from annihilation.

"Wait a minute," you say. "Jesus isn't an *unlikely* hero! I mean, He's *God*, man!" Well, if there's one thing that the "unlikely hero" element teaches us, it's that heroes only *appear* to be unlikely. In reality, they always turn out to be the perfect one for the job. The wise men expected to find a royal prince living in a palace. Jesus' followers and disciples expected him to be a warrior who would overthrow the Roman oppressors and restore an earthly kingdom. The baby in the manger who came as a servant and a sacrifice didn't quite fit their expectations. He wasn't the hero they were looking for, but He was the hero that they needed.

The very fact that God humbled himself to take on mortal flesh and be born of a virgin attests to his "unlikely" hero status. It's unlikely that there was anything extraordinary about his appearance, for the Bible tells us, "He had no beauty or majesty to attract us to him, nothing in his appearance that we should desire him. He was despised and rejected by men, a man of sorrows, and familiar with suffering. Like one from whom men hide their faces he was despised, and we esteemed him not" (Isaiah 53:2-3). Even today, Jesus is often despised or at least ignored by those who need Him in their lives. He just doesn't seem like the type who can solve their problems, much less save the world. He remains an "unlikely" hero because although you wouldn't guess it at first glance, He's the only One who can get the job done.

Many heroes in literature have royal or even divine heritage; Jesus has both. He is the Son of God, begotten from before all worlds. And He is the Son of David whom God promised would reign eternally. You won't find a hero with a lineage much more special than that! The Bible doesn't explicitly state how and when Christ as true man became aware of His own divinity, but we do see a "realization" of His identity as true God; that is, we witness His power becoming manifest through His miracles and preaching. There are many individual scenes from the life of Christ that we could point to as examples of His true identity being revealed. Ultimately, his identity as the "Lamb of God" – the once and for all sacrifice to atone for the sins of the world – is realized upon the cross of Calvary; and His identity as true God and victor over sin and death is realized at His triumphant resurrection from the dead.

When did Jesus receive the "Call to Adventure"? One could argue that it came before the creation of the world even took place, knowing that it would lead Him to suffer and die to redeem His lost children. Wherever we place it, there is no denying that God was compelled to leave his heavenly home and enter a world sullied with sin, death, and temptation. He left the "ordinary world" behind ("ordinary" for *Him*, that is) and set off to face the trials and obstacles of the new and dangerous world.

"Aha," you're thinking, "we've got him now. Most heroes don't begin their quest on purpose, and you certainly can't say that about Jesus!" While God knew full well from the beginning that the world would fall into sin and lead Him to suffer and die, that wasn't His original design. His plan laid out the perfect paradise of a creation with no sorrow or sin or fear. It was human rebellion that caused sin to enter the world. Thankfully, God saw all this beforehand and set into motion the most beautiful rescue mission of all time. So no, His coming into this world was no *accident*. But then again, it wasn't His purpose that we should fall away from Him in the first place.

The Bible is brim full of "crossroads decisions;" seemingly insignificant events that needed to happen "just so" in order for God's plan of salvation to unravel perfectly. All of the crazy encounters, the epic battles, and even the tragic exiles happened for a reason, although many of the Israelites undoubtedly thought they were the product of "chance" or "coincidence." Just as the hero sees at the end of his journey how every crossroads decision led him to the exact point where he was "supposed" to be, so we see how every Old Testament occurrence was laying the groundwork for God to achieve our redemption in the fullness of time. The crossroads decisions and all the other encounters and twists and turns along the hero's journey are just pieces of a much bigger picture, and sometimes the hero is fortunate enough to realize that there is someone at work behind all this. As Gandalf tells Bilbo, "You don't really suppose, do you, that all your adventures and escapes were managed by mere luck, just for your sole benefit?" So in the same way, every miniscule detail of the Old Testament is important to the overall work, and every event in Jesus' life is part of His plan for our salvation.

God *invented* foreshadowing. It's *everywhere* in the Bible; every prophecy, every messianic promise, every bronze snake on a cross, and every whale spewing a man up on shore after three days points toward the final showdown between Jesus and Satan. Jesus is constantly predicting and foreshadowing the true nature of his mission on earth, and the fulfillment of everything He says proves that His Word can be trusted. This means that we can *know* that our sins are forgiven. We can *know* that we are right with God once again. And we can *know* that He is preparing a place for us where we will live with Him eternally.

Protective threshold guardians mean well, but don't always see the bigger picture. Jesus' were no exception. Even His family didn't always get what He was all about, and at times this threatened to hinder His ministry (Luke 2:41-50; Mark 3:20-34). Peter tries to intervene when Jesus begins to predict His own death, and Jesus rebukes him severely; "'Get behind me, Satan! You are a stumbling block to me; you do not have in mind the concerns of God, but merely human concerns" (Mt. 16:23). Jesus needed to willingly lay down His own life in order to save us, and even those who were closest to Him had trouble understanding what His mission really was.

Of course, if Jesus ever felt a little too over-protected, there were plenty of dangerous threshold guardians as well; a wicked king who tried to kill him as an infant (Mt. 2:1-16). Pharisees and teachers of the law who would love nothing more than to serve up His head on a silver platter (Mt. 21:46; Mark 12:12; Luke 20:19). Demons who assaulted Him from all sides, panicking in the presence of the Light of the World but determined to hinder Him all the same (Mt. 8:28, 9:34, 12:22, 17:14; Mark 1:34, 5:12; Luke 4:33, 8:30). Even Satan himself confronts Jesus in a bid to undermine His quest (Mt. 4:1-11).

Most heroes decide at some point along the journey that maybe they'd like to rethink this whole "saving the world" business. This "Refusal of the Call" shows us their humanity;

we get to see that even the toughest heroes have their breaking points. But it also serves to remind us of the terrible difficulties that the hero is facing. It's easy for us to sit comfortably on the couch and read about the journey, but the hero is living and experiencing all the pain, anguish, and fear first-hand. And lest we take for granted the horrible consequences of our sin, we see Jesus pray to His heavenly Father in the Garden of Gethsemane, "if it is possible, may this cup be taken from me" (Mt. 26:39). Already, He is feeling the awful burden of our sin. He knows that the road ahead leads to torture, death, and the scourges of Hell, forsaken by the Father. But despite this, He goes on, "Yet not as I will, but as you will."

The first and third persons of the Holy Trinity frequently act as Jesus' "wise and helpful guide." The Holy Spirit descends upon Jesus at His baptism (Luke 3:27) and remains with Him throughout His ministry. Jesus turns frequently to God the Father as his guide, finding a solitary place and praying for hours at a time. Just as a guide provides strength, encouragement, and direction for the hero along the journey, so Jesus as true man seeks these very things from the Godhead. Just as most heroes lose the guide at some point and have to stand on their own, so Jesus is forsaken by His Father (Mark 15:34). Our Holy God shuns the sin-bearing Jesus, and the Father turns His back on the Son in the final hour. And so Jesus experiences the true torture of Hell, something that no other living mortal has ever tasted; complete separation from God.

Jesus' disciples, friends, and other followers are His "hero partners or companions." Though they don't always understand the true nature of His journey, they leave everything behind and faithfully follow Him. While they are in themselves a part of His work and mission here on earth, He surely receives some comfort and encouragement from their companionship. Jesus calls them His "friends" (John 15:13) and seems particularly close to Peter, James, and John, who provide Him with fellowship during times of exceptional significance or extreme distress (Mt. 17:1-9; Mark 14:33). His partners and companions even assist Jesus with the work that He has been given to do, healing the sick and telling everyone about the kingdom of Heaven (Mt. 10:1-32).

While Jesus doesn't seem to carry a physical "talisman" around (except perhaps His own human body?), He certainly has many "gifts" that He implements during His ministry on earth. His miracles are a powerful manifestation of His own divinity, and they give the people around Him a taste of creation the way it was really meant to be; without pain, disease, death, and (most importantly) without sin as He freely forgives those who seek His mercy. Jesus *is* the embodiment of the fruits of the Spirit, and His true nature is clearly revealed through His words and actions. Just as a hero's talisman represents something about his identity or abilities, so Jesus' preaching and miracles testify that He is the Son of the Living God who has come to restore the broken relationship between God and man.

Jesus "embarks upon the quest" when He leaves His heavenly home to walk among us as a man. He embarks upon the quest when He begins His public ministry. Or maybe He embarks upon the quest on Palm Sunday when He triumphantly enters Jerusalem, willingly walking into the arms of death so that He can complete the work that the Father sent Him to do. All of these work well, because in each case Jesus is setting out with full knowledge of the road ahead and the enemy that He will have to face. He knows the sacrifice that will be demanded of Him, and He continues forward willingly.

If you've ever looked a map of Jesus' travels, you'll understand how He fits the "seemingly aimless roaming" Hero's Journey element. Up and down, north and south, to Galilee, or Samaria, or Jerusalem; across the Sea of Galilee, then back again. Jesus' disciples probably thought His GPS was broken with all the wandering around they did. And He certainly faced plenty of trials and obstacles along the way with plots to arrest and kill Him, demoniacs challenging Him, crowds of people to heal and to feed, storms to calm, and everywhere lost sheep in need of forgiveness and renewal. But this was *vital* work! Just as the hero's wandering is essential to his development and success, so Jesus is preparing the region (and the world) for the ministry that will continue after His death and resurrection. Jesus touched the lives of the people He met, and when those people later heard the *rest* of the story – how He had come to die for them so that they might live – they were primed and ready; the seeds of the Gospel fell into the fertile soul of their eager souls and exploded into life. Within one generation, the news of His death and resurrection reached the farthest corners of the known world in an age without automobiles or airwaves or internet. Jesus' followers saw for the rest of their lives how important those three years of "wandering" really were.

The "Underworld" – a place of great evil and danger from which the hero may not come back alive. In a sense, Jesus entered the "underworld" through a stable in Bethlehem. His birth there marked the entrance into a place where the enemy would be seeking to take His life constantly. Here, the Holy One would have direct contact with the taint of sin and death. He would lower himself to mere mortality. And from the very start, Jesus knew that entering our world as a man would lead to His death.

But we can also look to Holy Week to find other "descents into the underworld." His very coming to Jerusalem was for the sole purpose to give up His life, as He told the disciples beforehand (Mark 8:31). Already, the leaders of the Jews were plotting against Him, and He knew this, yet continued on with His mission unwaveringly. One could also look at the scene in Gethsemane as an "underworld" scenario, with Jesus willingly walking into the trap that had been set by His own disciple. Or perhaps it was when He was being taken to the Sanhedrin, or to Pontius Pilate. Any of these instances mark a point where Jesus enters a deathtrap; the forces of darkness surround Him and drive Him all the way up the hill to Calvary.

And this is the point where the real "descent into the underworld" comes. Jesus faces His final hour abandoned by His disciples, forsaken by His Father, and scorned by the ones He came to save. He suffers physical and spiritual anguish the likes of which the world has never known, and the enemy is celebrating their "victory" all around Him as He dies. And then, He literally descends into the underworld, into Hell, and confronts the nemesis once and for all; the party is over, and the enemy realizes too late that Jesus is here by His own design and not by any scheme of theirs. The three greatest foes of mankind – sin, death, and the Devil – are all defeated and disarmed in one fell swoop. Jesus emerges from the underworld in power and victory.

Jesus had plenty of encounters with the "dark side," and it certainly never proved to be too powerful *for Him*. But what was the *first* encounter that we read about in the Bible? It wasn't the assassination attempt by Herod, or Jesus' temptation in the wilderness, or anything else during the life of Christ. For this, we have to go all the way back to Genesis chapter three, where we find the Deceiver attacking God by leading His children into sin and death. Here, the "dark side" proves too powerful *for us*. In our first encounter, we got smoked. We didn't stand a chance. Like the hero in the story, we realize that the enemy is just too powerful for us; something is missing, and we can't possibly defeat him the way things currently stand. Thankfully, the *next* encounter with the dark side will be fought by the *real* Hero. Being the sinless Son of God, He alone has the means, the will, and the power to overcome the enemy of man and free us from bondage.

Every hero is tempted or seduced into leaving the quest or even defecting to the enemy. Satan is no dummy; he knew that Jesus' arrival on his turf marked something really big, and he wasn't about to just stand by and watch humanity slip through his slimy grasp. God taking on flesh and subjecting himself to human weakness was so audacious, so unprecedented, so wildly reckless that it prompts him to do something equally audacious. He goes after the grand prize and tries to lure Jesus into worshipping *him*. If he could pull this off, finally his dream of cosmic conquest could become a reality. The prince of this world knew that Jesus came here to defeat him, but he figured that God's Anointed One could also be his most powerful weapon against his former Master. So he leads Jesus away from all help, weakens Him with hunger and thirst, and then exploits His humanity to tempt Him into serving the Father of Lies.

Scripture tells us that Jesus was tempted the same way that we are (Heb. 2:18; 4:15), so we know that this must have been a terrible ordeal. Jesus' humanity was a sort of "tragic flaw" that made Him vulnerable to the attacks of the enemy. But He resisted temptation, defying Satan on every point and taking the counteroffensive. He was not seduced by the Devil's lies, but stays the course and continues on the path of sacrifice – the path of the Hero.

His own humanity was a "tragic flaw" for Jesus not only because Satan could exploit it to try to foil the whole mission of salvation (if he could only get Jesus to sin, just once...), but also because it puts Christ in physical peril. A tragic flaw is any "defect" or other character trait that causes the hero come into harm's way. From Jesus' perspective, being mortal man was certainly dangerous business. As a divine being, He would never have needed to suffer pain or sorrow, and He would certainly have never tasted the bitterness of death or have been afflicted with the ugliness of sin. All of this was a result of His choosing to become perfect man, subjecting Himself to all the trials and temptations of life on earth.

But this "flaw" was only the *result* of a different "tragic flaw." His greatest "flaw" was the very thing that caused Him to assume the form of a man in the first place. It is the force that drove Him to give up His home in heaven and sacrifice His life for us. It is the very reason that He created us, even while knowing the terrible price that it would cost Him. Jesus' *real* "tragic flaw" was *love*. It was His *love* for us that cost Him His life. It was His *love* for us that brought on every bane and blight in His existence. It was this love than made Jesus the only One who *could* save mankind, and the only One who *would*.

Jesus is the author of life and the inventor of the "death and rebirth" motif. After man dies spiritually in the garden of Eden, God supplies life for him in the hope of a Messiah. Each and every human being was dead in their sins, and God promises new life in Him through the waters of baptism. Jesus went all the way to cross, suffered a literal and physical death, and was raised again after three days in power and glory. No more was He the "suffering servant" who was afflicted by the scourges of mortality and human weakness, but has now become the victorious King who would make all His enemies a footstool beneath Him – though they sought to defeat Him, they would only serve to lift Him up yet higher. He would return to the Father to be seated at His right hand until the time came for Him to come again in majesty.

As mentioned earlier, Jesus' own knowledge of His divinity and purpose is somewhat of a mystery to us. Even so, there are a few scenes from His life that demonstrate a "mystical insight or transformation of consciousness" pattern. His visit to the temple as a child shows that already at the age of twelve Jesus knew of His identity and perhaps of His mission as well (Luke 2:41-52). His baptism in the Jordan River exhibited His divine nature and membership in the Trinity to all who were present (Luke 3:21-22). But an especially spectacular change occurs at His transfiguration atop the mountain (Mt. 17:1-9).

Perhaps Jesus didn't gain any new "insight" during this scene, and His "consciousness" may have remained unaffected. But we can rest assured that the disciples' understanding of who Jesus really is changed a good deal after that. It has been an ongoing process for them to figure out Jesus' true nature and to understand how His actual mission differs from their misconceptions about the promised Messiah. In Matthew 16:13-20, God gives Simon Peter a beautiful revelation or bit of "mystical insight" with His confession of Jesus, "You are the Messiah, the Son of the Living God." How did he know *that*? Jesus explains, "Blessed are you, Simon son of Jonah, for this was not revealed to you by flesh and blood, but by my Father in heaven." What a cool scene!

Or we could take the scene where Jesus reveals His divine power to the disciples by calming the storm on the Sea of Galilee (Mark 4:35-41). The disciples are terrified of the deadly storm – bear in mind that these men had spent their whole *lives* working in a boat on the sea, and had certainly weathered many storms before this. But they become even more terrified when Jesus rebukes the storm and it calms instantly. They ask each other, "Who is this? Even the wind and the waves obey him!" The question is rhetorical; the disciples know darn well that the wind and waves would only listen to the One who created them. Their fear is a result of suddenly becoming aware of the fact that *God* is in the boat with them, and they just finished chewing out the Lord of all the earth ("Don't you care if we drown?!"). You can bet that their "consciousness" underwent a little transforming that day.

But the greatest "mystical insight" or "transformation of consciousness" that any of the disciples undergo doesn't take place until after Jesus has died and risen again. Then all of the pieces fit, and the disciples finally understand what Jesus' business on earth was really all about. This understanding comes through the Holy Spirit (that's right, it's *mystical* after all), and boy, does it change them! They go from cowering in a locked room to boldly proclaiming Jesus in the streets, heedless of their own physical safety or the threats of the Jewish leaders. They carry the Gospel message to the ends of the earth, and these men of formerly such little faith now battle forth for the sake of Jesus even to their deaths. And still today, God's Word is "mystically" and mysteriously breeding faith in the hearts of men and women, changing them one life and consciousness at a time.

There were many "physical sacrifices or losses" along the journey for Jesus, starting at eight days old with His circumcision in accordance with Scripture (Luke 2:21) all the way up to and even after His death. At the Last Supper, Jesus foreshadows the ultimate "physical sacrifice or loss" for the sake of others when He tells His disciples, "Take and eat; this is my body" and "Drink from it, all of you. This is my blood" (Mt. 26:26-28). In Gethsemane, Jesus sweat was "like drops of blood falling to the ground" (Luke 22:44). Jesus is then beaten, stripped, flogged, and forced to wear a crown of thorns before carrying His own cross to the execution site. The piercings on His hands and feet and the wound in His side from the soldier's spear remain with Him even after He rises from the dead three days later – they remain with Him even today. His wounds are lasting signs of the suffering that He had to endure for our sake, but also glorious marks of His victory over Satan. One could even say that the very fact that He rose again in the flesh and retained His physical body is a sort of "physical sacrifice," or at least a change in His being that was caused by the journey.

Although Christ never experienced a "loss of innocence" in the sense that He remained the pure, innocent Lamb of God throughout His entire life, His physical loss was accompanied by an equally great spiritual sacrifice. He underwent separation from God and the torments of Hell on our behalf. He bore the sins of the world on His own person and tasted the bitterness of death – something that Almighty God by rights should never have had to go through. Just as the hero gives up the "ordinary life" for the sake of those he is trying to save, so Christ descended from on high to bear our transgressions and infirmities in Himself. While His physical suffering was indeed great, I doubt it can compare with all that He underwent spiritually.

All of these elements from Jesus' life lead up to what He came to earth to do in the first place; to slay the dragon. Were the odds against Him? Not really, although it probably seemed that way to those who witnessed the events firsthand. But in all the Hero's Journey stories that we read and enjoy, we know that in the end the hero will be victorious despite the odds, because we believe in something much greater at work behind everything that happens. In God's story of our salvation, all went exactly according to His plan. The sins of billions of human beings were paid for by the work of one Man, and He delivered the crushing blow to the enemies of the Holy God. Because of Him, we are free to fight our daily battles with God's help, knowing that ultimately the war has been won and our place in heaven is purchased and secured.

Just as the hero returns to the "ordinary world" and passes his wisdom on to other generations, so Jesus comes into the hearts of His children in a very real and personal relationship. He is not a distant God, but a Friend and Brother who shows us the path to walk and gives us strength and encouragement in our many troubles. He takes our failures upon Himself, driving fear, doubt, and despair far from our hearts. The dragon is defeated and toothless; death's sting has been plucked out; our sins have been washed away. Yes, the victory is complete.

Chapter II
Magic, The Blathering: How to Tell Which Craft from Witch

"Magic" is undoubtedly the single biggest obstacle between Christian readers and good fantasy fiction. If magic is an element in the story, many Christians will immediately recoil, withdraw a silver cross on a chain from around their neck, douse themselves in holy water and look for the nearest "Torch and Pitchfork Superstore."

But that's *witchcraft*, right?! Some of the time, yes; and in those cases I wholeheartedly condone nearly all of the aforementioned reactions. But most often, any "magic" appearing in fiction is little more than an effective literary device and is far less dangerous to a reader's spiritual well-being than a *vast* majority of "non-fiction" you'll find in bookstores or libraries. In fact, it can often be a valuable tool for teaching Christian values.

In this chapter, we'll discuss how "magic" is often used in stories in a way that poses very little spiritual danger; oftentimes by authors who are openly Christian to intentionally teach moral and spiritual truths. We will also discuss "magic" that reflects the very real and powerful forces behind *witchcraft* that are at work in our world today. To help readers understand the difference and equip them to better recognize "bad magic" in books, we will briefly explore some of the belief systems in the world today that incorporate witchcraft into their ideologies. Finally, we will look at how some Christians unconsciously hold attitudes and ideas about God that actually reflect the influences of pagan religions – a phenomenon which demonstrates that fantasy fiction is rarely to blame for our misinterpretations of God and His will for us.

> *"Dear friends, do not believe every spirit, but test the spirits to see whether they are from God, because many false prophets have gone out into the world."*
>
> *~1 John 4:1*

Doesn't "magic" blur the lines between reality and fantasy?

In most cases, that assertion is absolutely preposterous. "Magic" is the most obvious element *separating* the real world from the fantasy world in the minds of readers! In fact, that's the very reason that many authors choose to use magic in the first place. As soon as readers see the elderly fellow with long white beard levitate across the river or shoot a fireball from his fingertips, they say, "Okay, this isn't *real*. That sort of thing doesn't happen in real life."

Fantasy is meant to *reflect* life, not be a literal rendering. It is an effective way to help people understand important concepts.

When Jesus would teach His disciples, He'd say, "Listen up: The kingdom of heaven is *like* this..." and then go on to tell a completely fictional story. He knew that a story doesn't have to be "true" in order to be "truth." In fact, fiction (even fantasy) can be the most effective means to convey a message about life, faith, or a difficult concept. We constantly draw comparisons between things that don't seem similar in any way on the outside, because we know that there's an effective connection underneath. If someone isn't familiar with an idea, we compare it to something they already know.

Here's an example: Fantasy fiction is like a paintball training exercise meant to help new soldiers understand the dynamics of combat. The cadets *could* say to themselves, "This has nothing to do with the reality of war. The ballistics are completely different from live ammunition, the weight of the gun is significantly less, and the bodily damage sustained from the impact of the projectile is minimal. In *real* combat, I'd be dead from getting shot like that. Besides, we're leaving out important factors like the trauma of witnessing actual bloodshed and the fear of pain and death, both of which make a major difference in a critical combat situation. I really don't see how this is going to prepare me for active duty, and I'm going to abstain from these exercises so that I don't become *confused* about what's real and what isn't."

Of course the soldiers in this exercise know that the conflict isn't "real." It is vitally important that they understand the difference between a training exercise and lethal combat,

133

because the goals are entirely different. The differences are there for the safety and survival of the cadets, who are trying to learn about combat in a safe and effective manner.

When the real bullets start flying, how likely is it that the soldiers will get confused and think, "Oh, they're only paintballs"? No, they will be thankful that they had the opportunity to prepare for the experience in a hazard-free training exercise. They will know how to maneuver safely, how to communicate with their team, and how to operate their equipment; things that haven't changed from the training exercise.

Just the same, magic serves a purpose to distinguish the fantasy world as a "training grounds" where the rules are different but the same valuable lessons can be learned. While readers are obviously not expecting to meet wizards throwing fireballs at them or being afflicted by a cursed ring, they know that many challenges await them in real life. The same courage that helped the hero in the story defeat the evil wizard will help the reader stand up for his faith in a school that doesn't foster a spiritually friendly environment. The same fortitude and patience that helped the

> *"Literature adds to reality, it does not simply describe it. It enriches the necessary competencies that daily life requires and provides; and in this respect, it irrigates the deserts that our lives have already become."*
>
> *~C.S. Lewis*

hero withstand the temptation and suffering that the cursed ring caused him will help the reader to withstand temptation or despair in his own trials. Although the situations and circumstances in the stories we read are often far-fetched, the outcome remains that we integrate the lessons, values, and character exhibited in the fantasy world into our own lives.

Magic should establish clear boundaries

Magic can serve many purposes in fantasy fiction. It may help the reader to connect with the story better by absorbing them into a world of rich wonder and beauty. It may serve as an analogy for real-life power, such as authority, charisma, or wealth. Or it may simply help to advance the plot sometimes. Whatever the case, for magic to stay on the "safe" side in fantasy fiction, it needs to fall clearly in the realm of *fiction*.

Since magic defines the fictional world more clearly, it would defeat the purpose to write a story that is *supposed* to be set in a fantasy world and uses rituals, rites, or other forms of real world witchcraft as its form of "magic." That isn't to say that this never happens; it does, and frequently. That is why it is so important to be able to identify and avoid literature that promotes the use of pagan demonic powers.

Magic is generally handled best in fantasy fiction when it isn't *explained* in great detail. If wizards are able to do magic simply because they are born with the ability, fine. Here in the real world, that isn't going to send me on a mad quest in search of forbidden knowledge. If an object has magical powers just because that's part of its nature, very good. This use isn't going to encourage anyone to look up rituals for enchanting ordinary items. The conditions under which magical powers take effect are so vague that they are clearly only there for literary purposes, and anyone who is enticed into witchcraft because of reading about this was obviously predisposed to the notion anyhow.

Authors like J.R.R. Tolkien and C.S. Lewis were founding fathers of modern fantasy fiction, and they handled the concept of magic beautifully. For them, magic was simply a part of the fictional world in which their stories took place. Because they invented worlds that were completely separate from ours, the laws and dynamics that governed those worlds were different. The way magic worked was similar to the manner that gravity, velocity, or electricity abide by certain natural laws in our universe. It was clearly *not* the real world, but only a "parallel" of it. The fact that elves, wizards, or other characters have magical abilities was no more out of place than the fact that in our world, fish can breathe underwater and we cannot.

Yet writers are notoriously striving for fresh, vivid details in their stories, and sometimes they look to their theory or system of magic as a place to provide this. Magic *can* be explained in detail safely. For instance, a story might have a magic broomstick that allows someone to fly on it every fourth Tuesday of the month as long as their shoes are on the wrong feet and they are wearing a necktie instead of a belt. Aren't those fun, fresh details? But they don't try to explain away the *origin* of the magic; where it came from or what makes it work. The story might even try to do that, by saying that an old woman used it to smack a wolf on the nose during a full moon after sweeping up spilled garlic. We're still leaving out the source of magical power, and that's just as well. While this back-story is drenched in bits and pieces of pagan folklore, most people would agree that these notions are so cliché and timeworn that their acceptance into pop culture has rendered them fairly harmless.

This is generally the reason why "fairy tales" aren't considered terribly hazardous by most people. The extravagant characters and outlandish events help place the story *clearly* in the realm of fantasy, safely removed from any real-world connections other than the moral of the story. "Magic" is just how things happen in that type of story, and what makes the weird, fun, unpredictable occurrences possible.

From whence cometh such strange powers?

Unfortunately, the good old method of letting magic stand for itself in a story and do its job silently is becoming scarce. With the advent of "fan-fiction," web-based fan clubs, "wiki-pages," and the like, the trend these days is to explain everything to death. There is always someone who insists on knowing *precisely how* a thing works, whether it's a lightsaber or a magical lightning bolt. This is where magic can get into dangerous territory.

In reality, there are only two sources of supernatural power in our world; that which comes from God, and everything else which comes from Satan. We see both forms of power manifested frequently in the Bible. Exhibitions of Satanic power abound in Scripture, from Pharaoh's magicians in the book of Exodus, to the witch of Endor in I Samuel, to Simon the magician in the book of Acts. These all show us that witchcraft is a reality in our world; any supernatural powers obtained apart from God are solely from the Devil and will serve only his purposes.

Conversely, we see far more numerous and more potent exhibitions of power on the part of God Himself in the Bible. Miracles, signs, and wonders show the direct intervention of the Almighty throughout His story of the salvation of mankind. Prophets communicate God's will to His

> *"Miracles are not contrary to nature, but only contrary to what we know about nature."*
>
> ~St. Augustine

people and reveal His promises to them through the foretelling of the future. God demonstrates His omnipotence through creation itself, calling into being planets, stars, and living things out of nothing. And of course, Jesus demonstrates the greatest power in the universe in the climactic cosmic struggle for the fate of the world; He breaks the normal spiritual laws by taking our sins upon Himself, dying, and then rising again in power and victory over death itself.

These signs, powers, and wonders – both from God and from Satan – *could* be taken by some in our world for "magic." If this is the case, then these powers are either divinely given through the Holy Spirit, or they are obtained from the Devil and his demons through rebellion to God. Those are the only two sources of power available for supernatural or "magical" powers.

So, does the magic in fantasy fiction come from God or from the Devil? Take the wizard, for instance, who is acting as the "wise and helpful guide" for our young hero in a certain story. He uses his magic to fight evil, to heal, to assist the fledgling hero on his journey, and to help save the world. This power couldn't possibly come from the Devil; after all, "How can Satan cast out Satan?" And yet, I wouldn't go so far as to say that all good wizards in fantasy have been given authority from God to perform miraculous feats how and when they see fit.

The original question lays down a false premise. In *our* world, all "magic" or power must originate, at the source, with either God or the enemy. But remember, in the fantasy world, "magic" is not necessarily "witchcraft" as we know it, because magic is part and parcel to the world in which the characters live.

If a story were written about a land that doesn't exist in real life where all the people had six eyes and two mouths, we would simply accept this as the premise for the "story-world" and move on. There would be no question about the "morality" of the extra facial features, because that's just the way things are in this story. Or if a story were written where some people can change their skin color at will, and others are able to burrow through the ground like moles, and still others utilize echo-location to navigate dark places, no one would condemn any of these things as "witchcraft" or find them morally reprehensible.

But really, how different are these strange abilities from the magic users of typical fantasy stories? Is it because the magic in fantasy fiction is too much like "witchcraft" in real life? There are many pagan spells, charms, and rituals, but I don't know of many belief systems in this world where practitioners go around blasting things with lightning bolts and fireballs – a practice that seems to be common among wizards in fantasy fiction. I doubt that many dark cults market themselves by convincing young people that they can teach them to teleport across the country, or summon a warhorse out of thin air, or lift boulders by pointing at them. No, our common sense tells us that those things are elements strictly belonging to the fantasy world, and while they're fun to pretend and dream about, they aren't a part of reality.

Jesus once spoke of the dangers of trying to fit together two completely separate ways of thinking. He said, "No one sews a patch of unshrunk cloth on an old garment, for the patch will pull away from the garment, making the tear worse. Neither do men pour new wine into old wineskins. If they do, the skins will burst, the wine will run out and the wineskins will be ruined" (Matt. 9:16-17).

When people try to apply "real life" explanations to the magical fabric of fantasy worlds, the patch never holds. They are two completely separate things, or at least they should be (the next section deals with the dangers created when they *aren't*). We can't expect to be able to apply the rules of our world – in which magic could only be power given from above or below – to a fantasy world created as a parallel to our own with its own physical laws and mechanics. The wineskin bursts; anything good that we could have obtained from the story is lost and our own understanding is sullied by the attempt.

True witchcraft in fantasy fiction

By now, I've either convinced you that most magic in fantasy stories is no more than a fairly harmless literary device, or you've decided that I'm a quack and quit reading four paragraphs ago. Now I'll risk undermining my argument so far by cautioning readers that there are *also* many fantasy stories which describe "magic" in terms of actual pagan witchcraft, brought over straight from our world.

Some authors feel that in order to lend their story an air of "authenticity," they ought to make their magic more "realistic." This is where we get into trouble with young people having difficulty maintaining the boundary between fantasy and reality. "Magic" in these stories is often based upon Wicca, Shamanism, eastern mysticism, and other occult or pagan beliefs and practices. The "spells" are often found in ancient grimoires and described in some detail to help "immerse" the reader in the atmosphere of the story.

> *"To deny the possibility, nay, the actual existence of witchcraft and sorcery, is at once flatly to contradict the revealed Word of God...every nation in the world hath, in its turn, borne testimony, by either example we attested or by prohibitory laws, which at least suppose the possibility of a commerce with evil spirits."*
>
> *~Sir William Blackstone*

Young readers find this sort of thing fascinating, and they revel in the feeling that they have access to some sort of "secret forbidden knowledge." Teenagers crave attention; the need to feel "special" or "unique" in some way - any way - is a powerful motivating factor in the choices that they make. What kid wouldn't want to have hidden powers, to be able to finally have a sense of *control* over the world around them? Who wouldn't want to be able to impress the others with a display of mysterious force? And the result can sometimes be that young people are slowly drawn into occultism because of their yearning for respect, power, or excitement.

It seems harmless at first; they don't see how it's hurting anyone and they're still going to church – maybe just reading non-fiction books about "magicks" or looking things up on the internet. A few experiments here and there, just for fun. But it's an opening, and all the Serpent has to do is get his head in and the whole body will easily follow after. Faith can be quickly eroded and shattered when a person walks willingly into the houses of darkness.

Consider how magic is being used in the stories you read or in the movies and television shows that you watch. There is a great deal of difference between the fantastic structure of magic in C.S. Lewis's land of Narnia and, say, *Buffy the Vampire Slayer*, which is set in the "real world" and prominently features Wiccan practices. The easier it is to believe that "this is real" or "this is possible" (which it *is*), the greater the threat that a person's beliefs will be influenced by what they are reading or watching. There is a profound difference between an exquisitely crafted fantasy realm that seems to "come to life" and the dark reality of satanic powers that are featured in many books, movies, and games today. The fact that these depictions of sincere witchcraft are labeled "fantasy" is a deception in and of itself.

Animism

Probably the greatest influence at this time on the systems of magic being used in fantasy fiction is "animism." Animism is the belief that *all* things in the universe – rocks, trees, people, stars, etc. – contain some kind of spirit or spiritual energy. It is a primary "theology" of many New Age religions, but the idea is nothing new in itself. Shintoism, paganism, Wicca, many tribal religions, and even some forms of Buddhism and Hinduism embrace this philosophy.

Many fantasy fiction authors use this concept in their writings because it serves as an explanation for "magic." They assert that it is the "spiritual energy" found in all things – living or not – that provides the force or power behind magic. While serving a convenient purpose in their fiction, they are also connecting readers with a philosophy that enjoys growing popularity in our culture, much to the chagrin of the Church and Christian parents.

What's so dangerous about this idea? Lots of things. First of all, the basic premise is that "God" is not a single entity, and certainly not the Triune God that Christians worship. "God" is everything; the trees, rocks, stars, and most importantly, *you*. This is an idea that definitely appeals to our egocentric, self-serving culture today. Eventually, the conclusion must be that I *am* God and can therefore do whatever I want without regard to others or any form of deity. I have raised myself to the highest level of existence (something we are naturally inclined to do anyway), and thus have fallen into the oldest and most primal temptation; to rebel against God and replace Him with *myself.*

This philosophy also lends itself to confusing the "creation" with the "Creator." We obviously need to be responsible with nature and care for the world that God has given us, but we aren't to *worship* created things. We are already bombarded with messages telling us to put "things" before God, and we certainly don't need another excuse to do so; especially one that "moralizes" such an action and endows people with a warped sense of piety for succumbing to this temptation.

> *"Some have been to the mountain. I have been to my knees by the side of my bed."*
>
> *~Robert Brault*

Another main tenet and natural result of animism is the belief in some kind of "reincarnation." When a thing dies or is destroyed, animism says that its "life force" or "spirit energy" goes out of it, typically into some kind of cosmic pool of energy. As new "things" come into being, spirit energy is drawn from that "pool" and placed into the newly "born" object or creature.

Nearly all philosophies and religions based on animism weave a theology of "good works" into their beliefs. If you are a "good" person and don't commit evil during your life, then your lot will be somewhat better in the next life. It gives the individual a sense of control in an otherwise chaotic and unpredictable world, and it provides a measure of control over society in general (if enough people believe this idea).

Animism and the ideas that flow from it conflict with much of what we know to be true from the Bible. God created all things, and then breathed life into man and woman, giving them alone out of all creation *pneumos*, or "spirit." It is only God who "animates" us and gives us both physical and spiritual life. At our death, we know that we will stand before Him for final judgment, and we know that we will be clothed in the righteousness that is ours through Christ; a gift of God and not a product of our own works. It is only this knowledge and the life-giving faith through the Holy Spirit that empowers and "animates" us to serve God and our neighbors out of thankfulness, having been changed and made alive in Christ through His Word.

> *"I am the way, the truth, and the life. No one comes to the Father except through me."*
>
> *~John 14:6*

Animism and its effects can be seen throughout our society and have found their way into mainstream culture, right down to cartoon movies aimed at children. While I admire the *Star Wars* saga for their great portrayal of "The Hero's Journey," I am somewhat wary of their use of animism theology in their explanation of "The Force." Like with so many other factors, one needs to be cautious and discerning when identifying spiritual threats in movies and literature and carefully weigh the positive aspects with the dangers involved.

Shamanism

Another "contribution" to dangerous portrayals of magic in fantasy fiction is the incorporation of traditional shamanism as a means of magical power. "Shamanism" is the idea that an individual must serve as the "connection" between the "spirit world" and our own world, and that spirits and mystical powers are channeled through this person (the "shaman"). Priests in many tribal religions act in this role, and it has its roots in the traditional belief systems of Native Americans, Africa, Southeast Asia, and even some local pagan religions in parts of Europe. If fact, even the ancient Greeks used the "shaman" concept for those who served as priests and oracles.

> *"For there is one God and one mediator between God and men, the man Christ Jesus, who gave himself as a ransom for all men – the testimony given in its proper time."*
>
> *~1 Timothy 2:5-6*

Apart from the obvious spiritual dangers associated with this belief (see Chapter I part 6: "Danger!"), Christians need to be aware of some of the subtle influences shamanism can have on our own faith. Shamanism places an emphasis on "ritual," something that appeals psychologically to humans, giving them a sense of control, security, and familiarity. It expresses a belief in the power of charms, trinkets, or other objects that hold "mystical" powers; a concept that the Church has tried to combat for centuries. It also places faith in human beings and their ability to interact with, coerce, and communicate with "God" or the "spirit world," rather than placing faith and trust in God and relying on His Word for guidance and revelation.

Occultism

The "occult" is a broad term that generally describes most belief systems that in some way counter Christian theology. More precisely, it refers to practices such as Wicca, Satanism, paganism, astrology, divination, alchemy, or any other belief system that purportedly relies on "secret" or "hidden" knowledge for supernatural or paranormal powers.

The individual methods and practices of each of these "religions" are too varied and numerous to detail in this book, so I won't. But what binds these groups together is the common practice of seeking knowledge, power, or advancement by means that have been forbidden by Scripture. God wants His children to rely on *Him* for guidance, protection, and wisdom. However, our lack of faith and sinful tendency to rebel often causes people to turn to created things for insight (the stars, magic bones, chicken entrails, etc.), or to seek knowledge from (evil) spirits. Again, refer to Chapter I part 6: "Danger!" for more explanation on this point.

Unfortunately, believers and proponents of the occult tend to be naturally drawn toward writing fantasy fiction because of their "esoteric" interests; much more so than most Christian writers. So readers do need to be on the lookout for occult references and influences in the stories they are reading. It is difficult for writers who belong to occult groups to avoid promoting their beliefs and "educating" their readers about their theological ideas and practices in the stories they write. It is the responsibility of the reader to understand *what* they are reading, know which authors have a reputation as dangerous pundits of the occult, and to be prepared and equipped to combat these influences in their own heart and in the world around them.

Danger!

Ah, fairy tales…

Every child clearly knows when something belongs in the realm of fantasy because of the outlandish occurrences and freakish phenomenon. I mean, come on; talking animals? Ghostly visitations? Dead people coming back to life? Obviously, these things could never happen in real life, right?

If you're on top of your game right now, you've realized that of course all those things *can* and *did* happen; we've read about them in the Bible. Unfortunately, our society looks at the inerrant, inspired Word of God as little more than a collection of fairy tales with the occasional dusting of poetry and history. After all, we've been so careful over the years to keep kids from getting confused about what's real and what's make-believe that they absolutely *know* that none of those miraculous events are possible.

While it's important to help your kids understand the difference between fantasy fiction and real life, it's even more important to assure them that what we read in the Bible is real *Life* (in fact, the Way, the Truth, and the *Life*). Many kids are read fairy tales when they go to bed at night, with their parents dutifully assuring them that it's all just pretend and nothing like that ever happens in the real world. Then they go to Sunday School and hear about talking snakes and donkeys, floating axes, people getting swallowed and regurgitated by giant fish, and pedestrian crossings in the middle of the sea. As far as they're concerned, it's just another fairy tale – and the world is right there to reassure them of that conclusion when they go to school the next day.

Make sure this is a major part of your conversations with your kids about the Bible and about fantasy. It's hard, but you need to help them to know that all of those improbable incidents in the Bible are one hundred percent true. Show them the beautiful way that each one points toward God's plan for our salvation through the life, death, and resurrection of His Son (because they *all* do – ask your pastor for help if you don't see how with some of them). Don't make the mistake of spending so much time making sure they know what *isn't* true that you forget to tell them what *is*.

Common Christian Pitfalls

Christians, even those who have never touched a fantasy fiction book in their lives, aren't immune to the subtle influences of witchcraft in the way they think and act. Christianity can be twisted and perverted by pagan practices that have invisibly worked their way into the fabric of our faith. Without even realizing it, people sometimes fall into habits that reflect ideas that are not at all inspired by God's Word, but rather by secular, pagan, or even occult messages and philosophies.

> *"For where God built a church, there the Devil would also build a chapel."*
>
> *~Martin Luther*

We sometimes fall into the ways of "animism," thinking that I need to "work my way up the spiritual ladder" and earn my way into God's good graces, forgetting that I'm saved by grace alone in Christ crucified. Other times, like "shamanists," we place our faith in objects, rituals, or other people instead of God alone, forgetting that "there is one God and one mediator between God and man," Jesus Christ. Sometimes, we even act like members of the "occult," reveling in our "secret knowledge" and forgetting that Jesus Christ died for *all*, and we have been sent to share the Gospel with everyone we meet.

The most prominent of these distortions today is what is commonly termed "prosperity theology." The basic premise is that people can "manipulate" God into giving them whatever they desire by saying the proper prayers, doing the right actions, or achieving the right frame of mind. This doctrine has enjoyed some popularity for the last hundred years or so, but has become increasingly popular since World War II and especially in the last thirty or forty years.

It doesn't require a real thorough inspection to see how this idea contradicts God's Word and reflects the pagan influences of ritualistic witchcraft. When God tells us to "seek first the kingdom of God and His righteousness, and all these things will be added to you as well," it isn't a recipe for fiscal success. God's will for our life is good and loving, and He desires that we be happy, healthy, and successful. Obeying His commandments and precepts naturally leads to prosperity, but not necessarily as the world sees it. In this sinful, fallen world, many Christians have to sacrifice worldly success for the sake of adhering closely to the Father's will. They are scorned and ridiculed for their faith, and some even lose their reputations, property, or lives because of it. Jesus warns that *persecution* will be a natural result of discipleship, not financial and physical well-being.

When we try to make God into a pagan deity who can be controlled and manipulated through silly incantations, empty rituals, and hollow servitude, we miss out on the most tremendous blessings He has in store for us. Our Heavenly Father wants *so much* for us in our lives, and not just sports cars, delicious foods, and fancy jewelry. He wants to craft us, to mold us, to make us more like Him, so that we can understand just how wonderful life can be when we walk together in unity – despite whatever suffering or difficult circumstances we may be going through at the time.

The prayer of Jabez in the Bible has been misused by thousands of men and women hoping for a "genie-in-a-bottle" phenomenon. That's fine. *Ask* God to bless you, by all means. But you should also realize that sometimes God blesses us through pain, loss, and sorrow. Sometimes He gives us the best things in life in a way that will make you want to curse His name during the process. Sometimes cancer will be the blessing you ask for, or unemployment, or loneliness, or any number of fears, doubts, temptations, heartaches, and tragedies. Because the greatest blessing we could ever have, and the thing God desires most for us, is to be closer to Him. Bless me, Lord. *Thy* will be done, not mine. Give me a stronger faith. Take away all trivial distractions and help me to walk with you. Amen.

Chapter III
Wizards, Necromancers, and Witches: The Good, the Bad, and the Ugly in the Ranks of Magic-Users

There are all kinds of special powers in our world. I don't mean powers like Superman's ability to fly and bounce bullets off his chest, or Spiderman's web-slinging, wall-climbing, super-spider-power package. I'm talking about the special powers possessed by each and every person; their God-given gifts and talents meant to be used to glorify the Lord and serve the people around us.

To some people, God has given authority, leadership, or political power. To others, He has given physical strength, agility, or talent. Some people are blessed with charismatic charm that draws people to them and helps them influence those around them. Still others have been given the exceptional quality of kindness and compassion. Some have intelligence, or wisdom, or courage, or resourcefulness, or faithfulness, or…

Yes, the list goes on and on. We are the stewards of these special powers, exercising their use with careful judgment. If these powers were turned from their true purpose, each one of them could be a deadly weapon of the enemy. The battlefield is all around us. How you use your weapons, your special powers, reveals to all who your commander is.

Spells don't kill people...

The absurdity of blaming a weapon for the death and destruction it causes has been pointed out again and again over the years. Imagine the opposite situation: a man praising the scalpel that was used in his successful surgery while ignoring the role of the doctor. Or little kids watching a professional baseball game and saying, "Gee, that bat is really awesome! It just hit a homerun!" Of course that's ridiculous. Nobody remembers the brand of paint that Michelangelo used to paint the Sistine Chapel or the make and model of the dagger that Brutus used to kill Caesar.

A "gun" is just a *thing*, an object with no will of its own. The same is true of a bomb, a knife, a sword, a lead pipe, a candlestick, or whatever. It is the person who *uses* the object that is responsible for the outcome of its function. Many chemicals can be used as either poisons or medicines, depending on their application. Yet we tend to think of poison as being innately "evil," and medicine as intrinsically "good." But in reality, it isn't either until something is *done* with it.

The same is true for magic in fantasy fiction. Magic is a powerful force in the fantasy world, and those who wield it represent individuals who hold considerable power and responsibility. They would equate with the guides and teachers of our world; the civic leaders, the judges, the professors, the celebrities, the pastors, the professional athletes. All of them have been blessed with potent gifts, and they have been given the free will to determine how they will use those gifts.

Magic-users are susceptible to the same temptations as those who hold power in the real world. There is always the enticement to use that power for personal gain; for glory, for the gathering of wealth, or to accrue yet more power and control over the will of people "under" them. No one will debate that power tends to corrupt even the most seemingly unlikely individuals. The more influence politicians have, the more pressure is placed on them to make decisions for reasons other than the good of the people. The more talent or ability an athlete has, the harder it is not to make it "all about me." The acquisition of power leads to a vicious cycle, eventually spiraling out of control as greed and lust for more power snowball with ever-increasing momentum. Sometimes the individual becomes aware too late of what is happening and wonders how it ever got so far; other times, they never even stop to think about it at all.

The "Evil Sorcerer" Archetype

There is a reason why powerful sorcerers tend to be corrupted by evil, and there is a reason why corrupt sorcerers constantly seek more power at any cost. They serve as a potent archetype in fantasy fiction, showing readers the dangers that come with power in any form. The "evil sorcerer" is the antagonist time and time again in stories from

> *"Power tends to corrupt, and absolute power corrupts absolutely."*
>
> ~John Emerich Edward Dalberg Acton

all parts of the world because it shows us something about the universal human condition.

The most dangerous enemy isn't any single all-powerful magician; the deadliest foe we are up against is the part of ourselves that wants to be God. We desire to exercise control over others, over our world, over everything we come into contact with; and ironically, we often sacrifice control over ourselves in order to achieve this. The "evil sorcerer" archetype warns

> *"Power is my mistress. I have worked too hard at her conquest to allow anyone to take her away from me."*
>
> ~Napoleon Bonaparte

readers against the consequences of succumbing to this temptation, and the Hero's Journey teaches self-control, discipline, and other effective strategies to combat this thirst for power. It takes a far greater power to willingly give up or avoid power that can potentially lead a person to harm others.

The evil sorcerer is cunning, crafty, and intelligent, but he doesn't always exercise very good judgment (obviously). His character is flawed from the beginning, even if the only crack was the willingness to put his quest for knowledge or power before anything else in the world. He will see this quest as noble and righteous, and therefore will he rarely second-guess his motives and decisions. What could be greater that the pursuit of knowledge, after all? And quite often, he will convince himself that control over others is ultimately for their own good. He has a "greater good" in mind, and the will of a few individuals, or a few million even, must not stand in the way of progress. The end justifies the means.

What the evil sorcerer doesn't count on is that one individual could gain the kind of power necessary to challenge him, and then be willing to give it away. Why anyone would possess that kind of power and use it purely for the sake of others, he will never know. And that's what makes the hero so dangerous to him; the hero falls squarely in the dangerous and terrifying realm of "the unknown." The evil sorcerer's whole life has been spent trying to conquer the unknown and quell the fear that arises from things beyond his mortal ken, only to have his archrival take the mysterious form of some "unlikely hero." And the hero will have powers that the evil sorcerer has never tasted and doesn't know how to counter; love, faithfulness, compassion, and the courage and willingness to sacrifice self for someone else.

> *"I am not interested in power for power's sake, but I'm interested in power that is moral, that is right and that is good."*
>
> ~Martin Luther King, Jr.

We can be certain that there are "evil sorcerers" out there in our world today. What a pity that they will sacrifice everything good in their lives and the lives of those around them for something that is no more than a poison to their souls. But we can also rest assured that the forces of good will always overcome the hollow, evil desires of these deluded individuals. Evil sorcerers have always met their match in the heroes that rise up against them; this is the way it is in fantasy, because that's the truth in reality.

The "Wise Wizard" Archetype

They are a rare but invaluable phenomenon; a priceless treasure to the community of believers and the world at large. Those individuals who hold astonishing levels of power and authority, *and* manage to resist the temptations that come as part of the deal, are hard to find, but thankfully they exist. They are often behind the scenes, faithfully teaching, guiding heroes on their paths, and standing between this world and the forces of darkness surging at the gates. The directly intervene in the cosmic struggle between good and evil, willing to lose what power has been given to them for the sake of preserving the well-being of others.

> *"I hope our wisdom will grow with our power, and teach us that the less we use our power the greater it will be."*
>
> *~Thomas Jefferson*

What sets the wizard apart from the "evil sorcerer" is, of course, their wisdom. The evil sorcerer views this distinction with derision. He sees the "wisdom" of the wizard as weakness, foolishness in fact. As far as he's concerned, the wizard only lacks the courage necessary to do "whatever it takes" to accomplish his goals. But the difference isn't the courage, it's the goals.

Like the evil sorcerer, the wizard always has a "bigger picture" in mind. However, his understanding of what is best for everyone is radically different from the evil sorcerer's. The wizard believes in the value and dignity of the individual, something that the sorcerer would never tolerate standing between him and his goal; the acquisition of power. But for the wizard, individual life, liberty, and happiness often *are* the goals for which he is striving, and excessive individual power is one of the greatest threats to these values. Often, his wisdom even causes him to stop short in his own search for new and greater powers because he dreads becoming the thing that he has dedicated himself to fighting.

> *"The attempt to combine wisdom and power has only rarely been successful and then only for a short while."*
>
> ~*Albert Einstein*

The wise wizard often works through others, finding and encouraging prospective heroes, sharing their knowledge and wisdom with those whom the evil sorcerer would deem "beneath them." For the wizard, the quest is never about "self," which is the exact opposite of the evil sorcerer. Even if he is the piece that brings everything else together, he knows that he is just one more piece in the larger picture.

Yes, the wizard is powerful. We are excited to see occasional bursts of power and magical strength, testaments to the true nature of the wizard. But he is reluctant to resort to these means except when absolutely necessary, which is an even greater testament to his character. He prefers to equip and empower others so that not everything rests with his own capabilities. He sees the potential in even the most unlikely people imaginable, helping them to become the heroes they were meant to be. So we see that the wizard's true power does not rest with his exceptional magical ability, but with the subtle wisdom that he uses to shape the future of the world.

The wise wizard is another powerful literary archetype. They are sometimes hard to identify in the real world (unless you've been privileged to witness one of their rare "bursts of power"). Nevertheless, we must not undervalue them. They are the quiet teachers, the elderly church members, the humble friends who never draw attention to themselves or their own deeds but inspire us to be something a little bit better. They are fierce to behold in a pinch, and can be relied on in times of peril as a powerful force for all that is good and pure and right.

These wise wizards are the ones we encourage to take on more power and authority but always refuse, recognizing the dangers and temptations. They prefer to quietly go about their business of guiding others, molding individuals instead of herding the masses. They are sculptors of human character and dignity, and shape our world one fledgling hero at a time. My plea to them is the same as that of the Elvenking to the wizard

Gandalf: "May you ever appear where you are most needed and least expected!"

The "Sorceress" Archetype

Male "professional" magic-users have somewhat more distinct categories based upon their morality than do their female counterparts. "Wizards" are typically good, "sorcerers" and "warlocks" are generally bad, and "magician" is a morally neutral term. While there are exceptions, these classifications hold true in most circumstances.

For whatever reason, the nomenclature for female magicians is somewhat ambiguous, especially in more recent works of fantasy fiction. Rather than engage in a discussion of the reflection of male chauvinism or the feminist movement in fantasy terminology, I will try to give readers some general guidelines and examples. (end of disclaimer)

While the term "sorcerer" for male magicians typically implies evil intentions and a mad quest for magical knowledge, female "sorceresses" vary widely in their portrayal. The term "sorceress" has little moral connotation in itself, and it is usually attached to "evil," "friendly," "wicked," "kind," or some other descriptive word to tell us more about her nature. Whether this is because women have been looked at as more mysterious and elusive than men, or serves as a subtle commentary on women in positions of power, or some other Freudian horse-hockey, I don't know (see above disclaimer).

But I *do* know that it provides fertile ground for a good crop of juicy literary archetypes.

The "Evil Sorceress" Archetype

The "evil sorceress" (sometimes called "evil enchantress") possesses extensive magical powers, but these powers are usually manifested differently than those of her male counterpart. She usually appears to be young and beautiful, often using a great deal of magic to keep herself that way. While males tend to value power and control, she is tempted into the misuse of her powers by vanity and narcissism. Her dwelling place is usually dark and barren, with few or no companions or attendants except possibly a handful of mindless automatons.

The evil sorceress excels in illusions and mind-affecting spells. Like the male sorcerer, she craves control over the world around her; but like the wizard, she focuses on individuals rather than large groups. Instead of guiding, teaching, and equipping heroes, she attempts to seduce, distract, and harness them under her own control. She preys on the flaws and weaknesses of the hero, breaking down the psyche and crushing any willpower to resist. Eventually, she will exercise such control over individuals that they will fiercely and loyally defend her against the very people who want to free them from her tyranny.

The evil sorceress archetype portrays a very special brand of sin or temptation. Like the fruit of the garden, some sins are just so "pleasing to the eye" that we indulge in them even though we know they aren't good for us. We nurse the illusion that "we are in control" and can "stop anytime we want to." In reality, we are being enslaved – mind, body, and soul – by a malevolent master. But we come to "love" that master so much that we even attack people who are close us when they try to free us from that sin.

> *"With persuasive words she led him astray; she seduced him with her smooth talk. All at once he followed her like an ox going to the slaughter…little knowing it will cost him his life."*
>
> *~Proverbs 7:21-23*

The evil sorceress uses deceit, cunning, and manipulation in place of the sorcerer's brute force. She is intelligent and crafty, but is extra dangerous because of the warped "wisdom" that she applies to her craft. In reality, she may not be very wise in the grand scheme of things, but she certainly *appears* wise and convincing to her victims. Heroes often need to rely on their partners and companions to resist her powers, and readers learn from her just how easy it is to become infatuated with even the deadliest of villains.

The "Good Sorceress" Archetype

> *"Power is not alluring to pure minds."*
>
> *~Thomas Jefferson*

The "good sorceress," on the other hand, is also typically fair to behold. However, her beauty does not come by the unnatural misuse of her magical powers but by the natural manifestation of her inner character. Her age is not usually magically concealed or altered, but it becomes muted and softened by her other qualities. She often resides in nature, surrounded by clean, pure waters and abundant life. These she strives to protect, defending a good, untainted world from the corrupting evil that is spreading abroad. Her home is a safe-haven for weary travelers and forlorn heroes, a place where they quickly recover in mind and body and receive good counsel for their journey.

The good sorceress is subtle, like her evil counterpart. But instead of the scheming, deceptive subtlety of the evil sorceress, she possesses a quiet, unassuming modesty. She is gentle and kind, seeking to heal and liberate where the evil sorceress would harm and enslave. She has an intuitive wisdom that rarely needs to be displayed in words. Often just being around her is enough to

> *"She will set a garland of grace on your head and present you with a crown of splendor."*
>
> *~Proverbs 4:9*

help people sort out their muddled thoughts, decide on the right course of action, and be inspired to move boldly forward through difficulties.

The good sorceress uses her power discreetly and effectively, much like the wizard. She models the Biblical portrait of feminine grace and wisdom, and shows readers how to meekly provide sanctuary to troubled spirits. She teaches us how to steadfastly defend all that is green and good in this world while maintaining the poise and dignity of our position. Like the Good Shepherd, she provides cool waters and gentle pastures for battle-weary soldiers. Seek her while she may be found, for her kind is quickly vanishing from our world.

The "Witch" Archetype

The term "witch" has historically carried a patently evil connotation. However, this has changed a great deal in recent fantasy fiction. Author L. Frank Baum, in his tales of *Oz*, breaks the mold by introducing "Glinda the Good" as well as the "Wicked Witch of the West." Since then, the question is always, "Well, are you a *good* witch or a *bad* witch?" The term is no longer morally prescriptive, and now we have "Sabrina the Teenage Witch" and all manner of young "witches" in J.K. Rowling's world of *Harry Potter* who represent equally morally diverse characters in the real world.

How do they differ from other female spellcasters? Sorceresses tend to be of a "loftier" nature than witches, often remaining aloof from the hustle and bustle of society. Witches, on the other hand, are frequently found right in the thick of things, where the action is. While they don't usually possess the level of magical power that sorceresses do, they tend to make much more overt displays of their power.

While evil sorceresses usurp magical power to keep themselves unnaturally young and beautiful, evil witches tend to be old and ugly – the classic representation of the witch as a hag with green skin and hairy warts on her oversized nose. While this is not always the case, the generalization draws attention to the fact that evil witches may have more in common with male sorcerers than female sorceresses. They are focused on power and the effects of their craft rather than their own physical appearance. On one hand, their lack of vanity means that they have one less "soft spot" exposed and don't fall prey as easily to attacks on their self-conceit.

On the other hand, evil sorceresses use their physical beauty and charm to lure and ensnare their victims; so evil witches must resort to other weapons and means by which they can overcome their enemies. This usually isn't a problem for them, since they generally prefer to take a more direct approach anyhow. Their exhibition of powers in flashy displays shows that they also can influence the minds of their victims, but do so through fear and wonder rather than seduction. Even their repulsive appearance adds to the "mystique" that they carefully nurture when dealing with society.

All the same, evil witches generally don't *intend* to become hideous, ugly creatures. The outward appearance is a manifestation of the corrupting evil on their inner character. Just as the good sorceress is surrounded by an aura of natural beauty that reflects her pure heart and soul, so the witch's evil will sooner or later show itself in warts, blotches, or other malefactions. It is a literary technique that provides the reader with a concrete visual for this particular archetype. However, the most hideous witch can often temporarily transform her physical appearance into a most beautiful exterior; something which readers also ought to take to heart.

> *"The soul that has conceived one wickedness can nurse no good thereafter."*
>
> ~Sophocles

While the evil witch uses her magic for selfish or often purely evil intentions, she cannot match the evil sorceress in terms of truly diabolical actions. Her schemes don't typically run as deep nor do they have outcomes quite so sinister in nature. She is dominated by incontinence, succumbing to greed and rage easily but not quite as willfully malevolent as the evil sorceress. All the same, she proves a useful minion in the forces of darkness and a considerable barrier to any hero's quest.

The "good witch" is not necessarily beautiful, often seeming mundane or even difficult to identify as possessing magical powers at all. They make frequent use of their magical abilities, generally to protect individuals in danger, heal or remove harmful magic, or to ward off enemies or evil forces. They are driven to use their talents in a benevolent fashion through their sense of compassion, justice, or virtue.

Good witches assist heroes in many ways. Their ability to heal wounds and remove harmful magical effects enables a journey that might otherwise be stymied or sidetracked to continue forward. They often have useful advice or wisdom that will prove useful later on, something that is mirrored by their use of protective spells and charms that stay with hero long after his departure from them. Above all, the good witch reminds the hero of the existence of benevolent forces in his world and the goodness in humanity that he is sworn to defend. Though their encounters are usually brief, they provide valuable hope and healing to the hero that will remain with him for much of the journey ahead.

The "good witch" archetype reflects those around us who are always ready with a friendly smile, an attentive ear, or a shoulder to cry on. They are easily taken for granted, but their assistance in our journey is critical to our success. When the world seems cruel and full of darkness and malice, they are there to remind us that some people still exist who will use their "powers" to help and heal instead of to tear down and destroy. They are a part of the world that the hero is sacrificing so much to defend, and their existence makes that sacrifice just a little bit easier.

The "Necromancer" Archetype

"Necromancers" are the most vile and loathsome of all the magic users in fiction. They use the rotting corpses of their defeated foes to reinforce their armies, commanding legions of skeletons, zombies, and other "undead" minions (see chapter IX if not familiar with this term). Their magic is dark and sinister, giving unnatural animation to dead, soulless vessels and spreading disease, death, and contagion among the ranks of the living. Often, they even use dark rituals to extend their own existence beyond the normal span of life, choosing to continue their quest for power and domination as a sentient undead creature themselves.

Traditional necromancy usually involved only contact or communication with the dead. It was the "art" of conjuring up spirits, invoking their assistance, or forming a pact with them to achieve some kind of goal. In modern fantasy fiction, necromancers have evolved to become representatives of all that is abhorrent and abominable in the realm of magic. While evil sorcerers use destructive magic for malevolent purposes, their powers are not usually seen as intrinsically evil. Necromancers, on the other hand, use magic in a way that is so contrary to the natural world that even many of

> *"I looked, and there before me was a pale horse! Its rider was named Death, and Hades was following close behind him."*
>
> *~Revelation 6:8*

their evil contemporaries despise them, or at least avoid dealing with them when possible.

Thus, the necromancer is often represented as the enemy of all. Unusual alliances and partnerships are formed in order to counter them when their power poses an imminent threat. Other grudges or grievances are forgotten under the threat of the armies of death itself. In an ironic twist, it isn't unusual for necromancers to be a catalyst for reconciliation and years of peaceful harmony after the threat is eventually contained.

The "necromancer" archetype represents the worst forces at work in our world; avatars of death and impurity. Just as the necromancer commands dead, rotting, and disease-ridden minions, there are certain sins or organizations in our society that are clearly unclean, fatal, and infectious (the Nazi party comes to mind as one sterling example). As the necromancer fortifies his army with the corpses of the deceased, so these forces in our world grow stronger through the destruction and conquest of any benevolent being or pure idea.

This archetype ought to teach our world, and especially the many denominations of Christians throughout the world, that sometimes working together in unity is necessary for the survival of all. God sometimes allows malicious threats to cross into the land of the living so that we may gain perspective on what is really important. While we may not agree on all points, we can at least cooperate to neutralize that which threatens our very existence; and sometimes a lasting peace will be the result. May we always recognize and resist these threats in Christian unity while there is still time to counter them, and may we always prosper together for years afterward so that the need for such an extreme measure to unite us becomes ultimately unnecessary.

Chapter IV
Weighing Dragons on their own Scales

While the pages of fantasy and mythology are teeming with fantastic foes and magnificent monsters, there can truly be no greater enemy than the dragon. Power, craft, and malice combine in these fearsome creatures to present the ultimate challenge to any hero. Their wicked ways, sly schemes, and brute strength make them analogous to many of the most terrible evils in the physical and spiritual realm of life.

In Western tradition, the dragon is a force of pure evil. *Beowulf*, one of the oldest works in the English language, pits the hero against a fierce dragon in an epic struggle to free his kingdom and preserve his own honor. This portrait of cruelty remained a template for centuries. J.R.R. Tolkien used this dragon as the model for "Smaug" in *The Hobbit*, and today the key traits of the archetypal dragon can still be seen in fantasy literature.

Dragons in fantasy and mythology not only teach us about the evils in the world around us, but also about the evils of the world *within* us. Sinful behavior is often categorized as "incontinence" (or lack of self-control), "violence," or "treachery," and dragons exhibit all three of these regularly. While fighting the evils that plague the world and those around us, we must also recognize and counter our own sinful nature. In the Hero's Journey story, the "dragon" is oftentimes the hero's own flaw – something which must be overcome before facing the *literal* dragon. As we study dragons, we are appalled and terrified because we see a part of them inside ourselves.

Dragons and Incontinence

While seen to be the "least serious" of all the human offences, sins of incontinence often turn out to be the small cracks or flaws in our character that lead to destruction later on. In *The Inferno*, Dante Alighieri outlines these malefactions as lust, gluttony, greed, and wrath; all of which can easily be seen in the ravaging destruction of dragons.

Lustful Behavior: The Dominating Dragon

While dragons are not usually represented as particularly sexual creatures, they do exhibit some "lustful" characteristics. Dragons have a peculiar habit of abducting fair maidens and carrying them off to their lairs. There, the distressed damsel is usually sullied in some way and – if not rescued in time – ultimately devoured. Why dragons would choose to do this when they have often just consumed a whole village of people is

> *"Jealousy, that dragon which slays love under the pretense of keeping it alive."*
>
> *~Havelock Ellis*

somewhat of a mystery. They could just as easily devour the maid on the spot and presumably save themselves a lot of complications, since many dragons have met their untimely demise at the hands of a vengeful or rescuing hero. But the desire to dominate the will of another singular entity seems to be compulsory for dragons, and this behavior has obvious undertones of sexual abuse or assault.

Dragons have a certain penchant for "purity" in their victims, often exclusively choosing young maidens of noble or royal lineage. This makes their act of defilement all the more abominable, since even if the girl is rescued alive, she is undoubtedly irrevocably changed by the experience. She often will have physical scars to remind her of the terrifying ordeal, although these cannot compare with the psychological and spiritual damage that her captor has inflicted by exposing such an innocent, sheltered victim to his dark and cruel deeds. The purity of the beautiful maiden is shattered, her innocence is lost, and often her whole being is consumed by the dragon's "lust," even if she has not been literally devoured.

Dragons do not confine their lust for domination to individual victims, but often terrorize whole villages or kingdoms by demanding a sacrifice; often of the aforementioned maiden. In this way, they are able to extend the life-shattering horror to every household and family, leaving each father, brother, and lover wondering if their loved one will be the next victim. It is the feeling of power and dominance that they crave; in much the same fashion as a rapist often thrives off of the sense of control over his victim rather than simply the sexual gratification. "Lust" is deeper than a purely physical affliction; it is a fissure that extends to the mind and soul, eventually cracking open and exposing the darkness within.

Just as a dragon's lust leads to the shattering of multiple lives and often to his own ruin, so sexual sins in mankind lead to all manner of heartache and serious temporal consequences. Often, lust is at the root of other sinful deeds as well, sparking off a chain reaction of destructive evil that ends in catastrophe. It is no wonder that our society has long placed such significance on this singular defect, and the permissiveness of today's world is a reflection of our own perversion.

The dragon shows the path of the hero. It shows that which he must overcome in himself to be the most effective at fighting the evil he is confronted with. Lust is the base instinct that most commonly afflicts people on their spiritual journey. Gaining control over this foe can lay the foundation for future victories, just as submission to it can lead to a spiraling downfall of despair and destruction. Don't rely on your own strength, but keep your sword sharp by remaining daily in the Word of God and seeking help from your partners and companions on this journey. The world would tell you that this battle is inconsequential, but it may be the most critical conquest of your adventure.

Gluttonous Behavior: The All-Consuming Dragon

Dragons aren't likely to coexist harmoniously with their natural surroundings. In fact, they usually consume, despoil, and destroy everything around them, creating an ever-growing radius of desolation. The most dastardly part of this conspicuous consumption is that it isn't necessary to the dragon's survival. It is part of their instinct or nature to consume as much as possible, leaving little or nothing for any other being.

Dragons aren't snackers. They are ravenous gorgers who devour whatever they can; more out of spite, greed, and malice than actual hunger. They are also lazy, seemingly existing for the mere purpose of eating and sleeping with the occasional outburst of violent destruction. They wake up every hundred years or so just to go out and eat a village full of people, or a whole flock of sheep. The size of the village or flock doesn't matter much; they eat until there is nothing left, then go back to sleep some more. Could they survive on only half a village? Or just part of a flock? Probably. In fact, they might just as well go on sleeping for another century without suffering any major side-effects from the lack of nutrition. But then again, their eating habits don't reflect a natural process designed for self-preservation. It is yet another way that their greed,

> "They whose sole bliss is eating can give but that one brutish reason why they live."
>
> ~Juvenal

malice, and lust for control flow out of their wicked hearts and into the world.

Moderation is a foreign concept for dragons. When they exhibit wrath, they do so excessively; Beowulf's dragon would have burned the whole world eventually to avenge the loss of a cup. When they hoard treasure, they can *never* have enough to satisfy their greed. They always need the most or the biggest or the best, no matter how impractical or even dangerous this might be. It doesn't take a real keen observer of the human condition to see how this relates to our own sinful nature.

This part of the dragon certainly resides within our own hearts as well. We ask God in prayer to provide us with "our daily bread," but take much more than we need, often to the deprivation of our neighbors. Many in the world struggle to obtain the bare necessities of survival, while we struggle to discover what luxuries we don't already possess. We grow accustomed to wallowing in excess, and then grumble and complain in circumstances where we have a little bit less but where God is still undeniably providing for us, richly and abundantly. We care more about our own *wants* than the *needs* of our neighbor, and we raise ourselves above God and His will for us.

Humans have not been faithful stewards of God's wonderful creation. We have often consumed resources more quickly than they are able to be replenished. At times we have expanded recklessly, heedless of the impact our cities are having upon flora and fauna. Our waste and pollution have contributed to creating desolations unsuitable for any kind of life. It matters very little to us how much we really "need" in order to exist in peace and happiness; if it's there, eat it, consume it, deplete it. We don't mind despoiling parts of God's creation if it means getting more of what we want. And the sad irony is, the more we obtain, the less happy we really are.

This characteristic of the dragon archetype shows us clearly the dangers of gluttony and excess. As the wasteland around the dragon expands, there never comes a point where he decides that he has burned enough forests. His appetite will always allow him to devour yet another city of men, elves, or dwarves. His treasure hoard will never grow so large that he finally decides that he has enough. Dragons are never happy with what they have, and will never be satisfied until *everything* is either in their possession or lies in ruins. That is their nature, and it is ours as well. A contented heart comes from knowing that all we need we have in Christ; that is the key to being "rich" in any circumstance, and is the best weapon we have against the dragon's gluttony.

> *"There are many things that we would throw away if we were not afraid that others might pick them up."*
>
> ~Oscar Wilde

Greedy Behavior: The Hoarding Dragon

Dragons love treasure. Though they haven't any use in the world for it, they cannot get enough of it. It is an extension of their gluttonous, excessive, compulsive nature to collect valuable things and keep them safely stowed away. Nothing provokes a dragon's anger like stealing part of its treasure hoard, as Tolkien says of Smaug in *The Hobbit*: "His rage passes description – the sort of rage that is only seen when rich folk that have more than they can enjoy suddenly lose something that they have long had but never before used or wanted."

The hoarding nature of dragons is one of the things that make them a particularly hated foe. They are the guardian that stands between the world and many wondrous and beautiful things. They are the barrier that blocks the path to wealth and prosperity; the treasure is useless to them but of inestimable value to the men and women of the kingdom. With the treasure, the king could feed his people, build walls for protection, or hire soldiers to defeat his enemies and restore peace and plenty to the land. The dragon's greed brings great enmity between him and world, instigating much bloodshed and violence on his part and often resulting in his own death when one hero is finally successful.

But alas, the trouble doesn't even end with the dragon's death. The chaos that ensues after the treasure's guardian is removed is entirely predictable and nearly proverbial. As soon as news goes out that the hoard is unguarded, all those within reach suddenly contract the "dragon-sickness," as Tolkien calls it. The cursed treasure results in so many wars, betrayals, and hostilities that the price in blood exceeds its total worth by far.

Dragon hoards are a reminder of the tragic potential that lies behind the promise of prosperity. They are a reminder that wealth always comes with a price. The human heart is capable of the same rage and bitterness over the loss of mere "things" that a dragon exhibits over the theft of treasure that is quite honestly worthless to him. Those around us can see what is most valuable in our lives by looking at where we focus our time and attention most, "For where your treasure is, there your heart will be also" (Matt. 6:21).

For dragons, a large treasure hoard is a status symbol – a measure of his own power and success. Dragons are exceedingly vain creatures, and much of what they do serves their own self-conceit. Flattery goes a long way with a dragon, and any decrease to the size of his hoard is a major blow to the dragon's ego (whether anyone else actually knows of the change is irrelevant). Somehow, his superiority over others is displayed through the heaps and mounds of treasure within his cave. After all, each item that he possesses is one more luxury withheld from someone else.

The greedy dragon emerges in human nature at an early age. Children will often refrain from sharing a toy simply *because* someone else wants it. They weren't *using* the toy or playing with it, it isn't something they've really shown much care for in the past, but now suddenly they cannot be parted from it. The logic is something like, "You want this. I have it and you don't. So I'm a better person than you." Any parental intervention and consequent compulsory sharing will undoubtedly result in fits of rage and a proliferation of tears.

This "dragon-sickness" grows steadily worse as the years progress. We are reluctant to get rid of or give away items that haven't been used in years because we just like having them around. We feel that parting with the item will result in guilt directed at ourselves for depriving ourselves of such a treasured possession. Most homes have at least several items stocked somewhere that have been purchased and never taken out of the shiny plastic wrapping that they first came in. We constantly amass more material possessions so that we can feel better about our standing within the neighborhood, the community, and in life in general.

Dragons, like us, are of the mentality that "he who dies with the most toys wins." However, dragons don't *really* plan on ever dying, although it inevitably happens anyhow. Humans don't have nearly the longevity of dragons, and when we focus so much attention on the trivial material pleasures of this transient life, it shows a serious lack of spiritual foresight. Just beyond the quivering boundaries of this mortal life, we have an eternity to either enjoy or lament.

> *"I have held many things in my hands, and I have lost them all; but whatever I have placed in God's hands, that I still possess."*
>
> *~Martin Luther*

Let us invest a bit more time and energy into stocking up on the oil of faith through the Word of God, and our worldly goods and treasures will suddenly seem much less valuable. The dragon of greed will be removed from the lair, and our wealth can be used properly to meet the needs of those around us.

Wrathful Behavior: The Raging Dragon

"...the worm came once again, murderous monster mad with rage, with fire-billows flaming, its foes to seek..."~Beowulf

The dragon's wrath is fierce to behold. With all its poise and cunning, it is sometimes easy to forget that the dragon is also a monstrous brute whose raw strength can shatter stone. When aroused to anger, the dragon holds nothing back. Flame pours from its snapping jaws while claws and tail rend earth, steel, and flesh.

> *"Men often make up in wrath what they want in reason."*
>
> *~William Alger*

As with all of the sins of incontinence, the dragon's wrath often leads to his own demise. These traits are all weaknesses, not only of character but of physical defense and security. People would probably have been perfectly content to leave the dragon alone in his lair, but his dangerous outbursts of wrath cause a hero or group of adventurers to seek his life. It is then his wrath that causes the dragon to "lose his head" (literally and figuratively), forgetting to protect himself in battle because his only thought is the destruction of his enemy.

A dragon's wrath stems from his vanity; any attack on his body, any theft of his property, any insult to his person in any way drives him into a towering rage. In this state he is extremely dangerous, but also reckless and often heedless of his own vulnerability. However, one thing is certain; there will be massive collateral damage when he unleashes his fury.

It's not uncommon to see this same display in people, especially in young men. They've got something to prove; nobody makes a fool out of them. They feel indestructible, and any consequences or threats to their own safety are a distant dream as they pour out their fury upon the object of their wrath. If temporarily thwarted in their retribution, their anger doesn't cool but rather builds like the pressure inside a boiler. A logical assessment of the situation would probably show that their rage is disproportionate to the wrong that has been done to them, and they will gain very little of useful value from vengeance. But any logic, any wisdom, any practical insight is lost at this point; consumed by the fires of their own hatred.

That's not to say adults are immune to this syndrome, by any means. How many businesses, churches, schools, communities, or families have been torn apart because of someone's pride? A perceived wrong was committed, and the "victim" will not rest until he or she has recovered their dignity; which usually means that every person involved will suffer retribution equaling ten times the original hurt. The result is generally one of two things; either the storm passes leaving everything in ruins and the wrathful avenger still is not satisfied, or the act of vengeance provokes further retribution from the other parties, leading to a vicious cycle of resentment, hatred, and bitterness.

Wrath is the last of the sins stemming from a serious lack of self-control. All of the sins of incontinence result from being unable to get a handle on "what *I* want." Lust, wasteful gluttony, selfish greed, and uncontrolled wrath all focus on my own desires without any thought for the needs of others or the will of God. It is the worship of *self* that makes these sins so prevalent in our lives, and the dragon is a striking example of how each one can cause utter devastation in the world. Falling into these temptations is a sin of the flesh; ignoring or justifying them is a sin of the intellect or will.

These sins of incontinence not only cause suffering and heartache for those around us, they are all ultimately self-destructive. All of them easily form into habits, causing us to daily place more focus on ourselves and less attention on God and those people He puts in our lives. They cause despair, driving a wedge between us and our Heavenly Father, preventing us from coming to Him in prayer and Scripture or from worshipping because we feel guilty and unworthy. They expose us to further attacks from the Devil and our sinful flesh, leading down a gradual path of temptation that takes us away from God and the good life that He had intended for us. Just as all of these characteristics of the dragon serve as vulnerabilities that can be exploited, so the Devil uses these parts of ourselves to cleverly attack and subdue us in our "moments of weakness."

Dragons and Violence

Apart from being sullied with all manner of personal moral flaws, dragons are willfully and intentionally violent. Sometimes their destructive tendencies don't even stem from their wrath. It is the dragon's nature to destroy, kill, and burn simply because it *wants* to. It is a *pleasure* to cause pain and devastation, and the dragon does so willfully and intentionally.

For most people, violence is a horrible thing. To see another person being physically hurt or killed is a shocking experience, something that leaves lasting emotional repercussions. Those for whom this is not the case should be seeing a good psychologist. Actually, they should be seeing the Wonderful Counselor, because our reaction to the pain and suffering of others is an indication of our own spiritual health. If a person has even an ounce of love or compassion for those around him, he will feel some measure of sympathy when he sees them suffering.

This is not the case with dragons. They don't care about anyone but themselves, and their depravity is of such a twisted degree that they perversely enjoy watching (and causing) pain and death. Believe it or not, there *are* actually people like that in the world. Scarier yet, that potential lies within our own sinful nature, and we all have the capacity to inflict harm upon those who oppose us. Most of us don't act upon these instincts (thanks largely to the "sword" of the government), but we have all certainly thought or wished harm upon others at some point. Perhaps it was someone at work, or a mean kid at school, or even just a careless driver on the way home. But the Bible clearly states that whoever hates another person has murdered them in their heart.

> *"Some men just want to watch the world burn."*
>
> ~Alfred Pennyworth: *The Dark Knight*

Whatever our own reasons or false justifications, violence in thought, word, or deed is yet another way that the dragon manifests himself in us. And the dragon makes no pretense about feeling guilt or remorse for what he has done; in fact, he boasts about it. Dragons are often heard bragging about how many villages they have destroyed, how many dwarves they have eaten, and how many maidens have been sacrificed to them over the years. It reflects again on their vanity; a flashy show of strength to remind themselves that they are the most powerful, the most feared, and the most hated.

This attitude leads to another kind of violence; violence against God. Dragons are blasphemers, through and through. They put themselves above anything and everything else in the world, and would never acknowledge that someone could be more powerful than they are. They breathe out threats and challenges to all those around them, trusting in their own strength to help them prevail in their evil deeds. Like Goliath the Philistine, they fear neither God nor man because they have deluded themselves into believing that they are the pinnacle of strength and power. And for their arrogance and blasphemous words, God uses the meek, the lowly, the "unlikely" hero, to bring down these colossal braggarts. The dragon trusted in the wisdom of the world: "How strong my body is! How sharp my claws and fangs are! My breath is a deadly inferno, and my scales are better than any armor! Nothing can defeat me, and no one is stronger than I am!" But the wisdom of God is shown to be superior once again, though the world would count it foolishness and put the odds on the dragon every time.

Pain, suffering, and death are the results of the curse of sin in the world. As avatars of destruction, dragons tear down creation and help to defile the good world that God created for us. The depredations of dragons are a natural consequence of living in a fallen world, and their tragic misdeeds become a part of everyday life for us. The world will never exterminate the dragon or be rid of his violent ways.

And yet, God gives us hope even in all of this. When the dragon rears his ugly head and spouts fire and brimstone,

God's warriors stand ready. When the dragon's destruction and blasphemy seem to be at their worst, God raises up a hero to defend His children. Jesus Christ won the ultimate victory over The Dragon, and that gives us the courage and strength to battle other dragons in our world and to overcome the dragon in our own hearts. Torture and cruelty will not go unnoticed, and the warriors will beat back the fiery beast until he is driven from the land. They will not let down their guard, but be ready to fend him off whenever he dares to sail over the plains or land on the mountaintops once more.

Dragons and Fraud or Treachery

Dante considered "sins of the flesh" (that is, incontinence) to be the least serious because we are more prone to them through our carnal instincts. "Violence" was more serious because it was an act of the will, and our intellect is a necessary part of that action. But he deemed the sins of fraud and treachery to be the most serious. Mankind has been given the unique gift of intelligence, and to willfully use that gift of God in order to harm others through *deception* is universally looked upon as utterly vile.

Dragons live for a very long time, and through all of their experiences they obtain some degree of wisdom. This is not the Godly wisdom of the wizard or "good sorceress" archetype, it is the cunning, crafty intellect of one who has seen many types of people and knows how to manipulate them. This aspect of

191

the dragon is what makes it a particularly deadly enemy. It has the size and power of a brute beast, a patently evil character, as well as the ability to use sense and logic in its destructive schemes.

Despite their loathsome reputation and fearsome appearance, dragons can be quite charismatic when they are working an angle. Silver-tongued villains have a way of controlling the minds of their audience. Even when they obviously desire nothing but harm for their

> *"Fraud is the homage that force pays to reason."*
>
> *~Charles Curtis*

victims, these smooth-talking worms can make an unsuspecting listener believe they are really their friend. Bilbo Baggins discovered this when conversing with Smaug: "Whenever Smaug's roving eye, seeking for him in the shadows, flashed across him, he trembled, and an unaccountable desire seized hold of him to rush out and reveal himself and tell all the truth to Smaug. In fact he was in grievous danger of coming under the dragon-spell."

It takes great skill and cunning to convince a sworn foe that you are really their friend. Of course, they probably can't *really* be convinced, but you can make them *want* to believe it. Our "itching ears" have a tendency to listen for the types of things that we want to hear. The adversary knows what we desire deep down; dragons have dealt with humans for centuries, and no one naturally knows better the depths of human depravity than a dragon anyway. He smoothly sows discord, suspicion, and doubt in our minds, and suddenly the dragon almost seems more trustworthy than our "friends." That is what Smaug does to Bilbo: "Now a nasty suspicion began to grow in his mind... That is the effect that dragon-talk has on the inexperienced. Bilbo ought to have been on his guard; but Smaug had rather an overwhelming personality." Dragons are false counselors, feeding lies into the minds of men for their own purposes or so that they can lure them to their death.

The hypnotic nature of dragons shows that they use any and all means to deceive their adversaries. They present their lies in such a convincing, persuasive way that even if people don't believe it, they still feel compelled to do what the dragon says. Just the same, many young people buy into lifestyles and philosophies that they don't really believe in, but they've been convinced that it's the thing to do anyway. *Truth* is irrelevant; they think that what they believe in their heart and what they do with their hands are two completely separate things. God says that they should lead a pure and chaste life, but the world is showing them something completely different. If the Devil can convince them that they can *believe* what God says while *doing* what the world says, he's got them under the dragon-spell. They *know* what's right, but like a zombie they continue to walk straight into the dragon's den as if they have no control over their own body.

Like the evil sorceress archetype, the dragon is a master of deception. He uses enticement, hypnotic talk, disguise, voice mimicry, and even illusion to convince enemies that he is someone or something other than what he really is. While capable of confronting foes with a head-on approach using raw strength, dragons prefer to use their wit to craft subtle treacheries and exercise control over their victims. This mental manipulation gives the dragon an absurd sense of pleasure and further feeds its already inflated ego. If there was ever any question about whether dragons are simply victims of sinful impulses, it is answered by their intentionally wicked use of violence and stratagem.

> *"When you betray somebody else, you also betray yourself."*
>
> *~Isaac Bashevis Singer*

Dragons in Eastern Tradition

It is interesting to note that while the dragon is looked at by most as a "fictional" or "mythical" figure, they exist as cultural elements in almost every part of the world. It's hard to say for certain whether this is because they perhaps existed in a very real and physical form at one time and are now extinct or hidden, or because the spiritual existence and influence of the "dragon" is imprinted on the hearts of all mankind, or for some other mysterious reason. All we know for sure is that the dragon has played a part in the shaping of philosophies the world over, and it has been interpreted in different ways by various groups of people.

In some parts of the world, particularly in eastern countries, the dragon is still seen as being powerful and intelligent, but is often viewed as a benevolent force. They are avatars of mystical power, of nature, and of the spiritual world. Eastern cultures and religions revere dragons for their wisdom and ability to unlock the secret things of our existence.

Naturally, Eastern culture and religion interpret "the dragon" differently because they have a different understanding of mysticism, nature, and spirituality. Remember that the dragon is a master of fraud and treachery, and he counterfeits many faces and shapes to trap his victims. Satan has never scrupled to lie about his name or true nature, often going by pseudonyms; Baal, Molech, Asherah, Shiva, Zeus, Ra, Thor, Wakanda, Mammon, Great Spirit, Essence of the Universe – in short, anything that people are foolish enough to worship and place before God in their hearts. He has today's world so befuddled that he needn't even use a name; he just whispers into people's ears, *"You ARE God..."*

Since the dawn of time, Satan, the Dragon, has been able to make others believe that he is truly wise – wiser than God, even. How else would he convince one-third of the host of heaven to rebel with him? It is how he persuades victims into following the path of self-destruction, even though they have been warned by God and loved ones not to walk down that road. He whispers, *"YOU know better than them. It's YOUR life; don't listen to them."*

So yes, to a culture firmly in the iron grasp of a pagan religion, the dragon would appear very wise. That is the face that he reveals to them, and that is what they are itching to hear. Because in our hearts, the dragon is also a part of *us*, and we deeply desire to do what he tells us. Ironically, when we succumb to the desires of "self," we aren't doing what's best for us at all. We are merely aiding the Dragon in *his* will, which seeks nothing but to devour us; mind, body, and soul.

> *"For Satan himself masquerades as an angel of light. It is not surprising, then, if his servants masquerade as servants of righteousness."*
>
> *~1 Corinthians 11:14-15*

Dragons: The Ultimate Archetype of Evil

Western literature has long seen the dragon as a symbol for all that is wicked in the world and in human nature. The Bible refers to Satan, the father of lies, as "the dragon." Thus, the dragon figure in literature and culture becomes a universal symbol for all manner of sinful behavior and distorted philosophy.

"Slaying the dragon" has long been synonymous with overcoming a powerful evil force. The appearance of the dragon marks a sudden shift from peace and prosperity to turmoil and suffering. All that was once green and fair and good is burnt away, a foul vapor rolls forth from the dragon's lair, and famine and pestilence reign as the land becomes inhospitable for life. Fear seizes the people in the surrounding countryside, and they live in constant terror of the sound of beating wings and the sight of flames leaping up on the horizon. Where the dragon reigns, there can be no light.

So we find him lurking in the darkness of *our* world as well. As sins of the flesh go unchecked and unchallenged (even encouraged), his power swells. As violence increases in our hearts, on our television sets, and in the streets, his fangs are bared and his claws are sharpened. The awful carnage left behind by his bloodlust can be seen in the daily assaults, riots, and shootings that seem to be ever-increasing. The strength of his fraud and treachery is so overwhelming that even our leaders, politicians, and judges have fallen victim to the "dragon-spell" and have mistaken virtue for vice.

In this climate of terror, it would be easy for God's people to cower amongst themselves and stay safely hidden away. They are tempted to think that if they leave the dragon alone, maybe he will stay sleeping, or at least keep away from their community. All the while his power is increasing and his desolation spreads farther and farther. New victims are devoured daily because no one brought them light and hope; no warrior dared to enter the dragon's den to free them from the bondage of their sin.

These themes, symbols, and archetypes exist in literature so that our young people will learn to never make this mistake. We read these stories so that we can better see what is really happening in our own world and be prepared to stand up against it. The dragon *is* powerful, but God always prepares His warriors through the trials and obstacles that they face. They need the courage to move forward. They need the hope of victory. They need the Gospel of Jesus Christ, for He is our Sword and our Shield, our Fortress, our Light, our Path, and our Captain. It is only through His death and resurrection that we find the strength to battle on, bringing that same message to all those living in the dominion of the dragon. For through this Gospel his power has been shattered; the fires of the dragon have been quenched forever, the sting of his fangs and claws is blunted and lost, and his scaly armor lies glittering on the floor, leaving him naked and vulnerable. Very soon, our King will return, take up the Sword of the Spirit, and strike the final deathblow to the enemies of man. Let us hasten to bring His light to all those who are still in darkness and desolation, that they may be found in allegiance to our King and Lord when he comes again.

> *"The great dragon was hurled down – that ancient serpent called the devil, or Satan, who leads the whole world astray. He was hurled to the earth, and his angels with him."*
>
> *~Revelation 12:9*

Chapter V
The Sword and the Warrior: Getting Medieval on Evil

I don't care who you are or how old you may be, there's something about swords that's just stinking cool. But there's something more than the sword's "awesome factor" that has caused it to be such a prominent part of literature over the centuries. The sword is an icon, a symbol that is steeped in heroic tradition and drenched with literary and spiritual symbolism.

Let's face it; none of us can resist wandering into that store at the mall with all of the cool medieval weapons (or at least peeking in through the window when we think no one is watching). Battle-axes, spears, daggers, flails, and the like all make for fun additions to any fantasy enthusiast's armory. And yet, there's something about the sword that fascinates us above and beyond the novelty of the other armaments. Grasping it by the handle, drawing it from the scabbard, the singing sound of the blade ringing in the air; a shiver runs down the spine and a surge of

> *"I don't do a film unless it has a sword in it. And if it doesn't have a sword in it, I insist that they have one in the same room to keep me comfortable."*
>
> ~Orlando Bloom

heroism floods the veins. We intuitively *know* that there is something special about this piece of metal before us.

The "Sword of the Spirit"

The Bible makes use of sword imagery many times, even using it to describe Scripture. Paul calls the Word of God the "Sword of the Spirit" (Eph. 6:17), and another epistle says that it is even "sharper than any double-edged sword" (Heb. 4:12).

Swords cut things. Hit a watermelon with a sharp sword, and it will open right up, revealing everything hidden beneath the rind. Hit a human being with the "Sword of the Spirit," God's Word, and it will pierce his flesh and bone straight to his very soul. It lays open our hearts and exposes that which is inside of us for all to see, whether it be black and rotten or alive and pure. With God's Word, we go under the knife, dissecting ourselves in a spiritual exploratory surgery to uncover the cancer of sin. And God's Word also has the power to remove that cancer. The Law shows us our sin and drives us to repentance, and the Gospel assures us of the forgiveness of sins purchased by the blood of Jesus Christ.

Sadly, because of sinful human nature this Sword of the Spirit will also divide households. Jesus told His disciples, "Do not suppose that I have come to bring peace to the earth. I did not come to bring peace, but a sword. For I have come to turn 'a man against his father, a daughter against her mother, a daughter-in-law against her mother-in-law – a man's enemies will be the members of his own household'" (Mt. 10:34-36).

The message is tragically clear; not everyone who hears the Law will obey it, and many who hear the Gospel will reject it – along with the one who brings it to them. Families will be divided over it, and people will be forced to choose between God and their siblings or parents. Communities will suffer division, nations will go to war, and the people of the world will struggle against God's Truth that came down and died for them. Unfortunately, they will literally take up the sword against the message of life that we bring; and our only Sword will remain the Word of God. But our Sword is stronger, and it will prevail.

God's Word is a mighty weapon against the forces of darkness in this world. When God speaks, powerful things happen, and He has been gracious enough to give *us* His Words and their power in our time. Ultimately, Jesus will return and conquer all our enemies by His Word; "out of his mouth came a sharp double-edged sword. His face

> *"The Devil fears the Word of God. He can't bite it; it breaks his teeth."*
>
> ~Martin Luther

was like the sun shining in all its brilliance" (Rev. 1:16). Sin, death, and Satan will be brought down under his sword of judgment and the nations of the world will be divided by it unto either eternal life or everlasting death.

Until that time, the Word of God is the Sword in our hands to fight for the souls around us. We are His chosen heroes, and He sends us on a difficult journey to battle the Dragon that rules this world. Though we are weak, His Word is strong, and it will endure all of the blows we receive and parry all the jabs of the enemy. Jesus Christ *is* the Word made flesh; if we have the Sword of the Spirit, we also have Him. And He's *more* than a match for any obstacle we might encounter along the way. What a privilege to see Him win our battles for us!

A Weapon of Divine Inspiration

Mankind is always inventing new weapons. The first weapons were probably just tools or ordinary objects until someone realized that they had the potential to cause bodily harm. It didn't take long for someone to find a need to inflict bodily harm (Gen. 4:8). If an axe is useful for chopping down a tree, why not for chopping down a man? If a rock can break open a nutshell, why not someone's head? And so forth.

Soon enough, killing became such a thriving industry that people devoted time, talent, and money to perfecting their methods of inflicting bodily harm by applying science and technology to warfare. Of course, with each new weapon came the demand for something just a little bit "better." And ever since, weapons have been constantly "improving" as mankind devises new and better ways to kill other human beings faster, more efficiently, and in larger quantities.

So all the weapons throughout history have been "discovered" or invented by human hands; all except one. I think we get chills running up our spines when we hold the hilt of a sword because something inside us recognizes its perfection, its beauty, its divine symmetry. It is the first and most perfect weapon, the weapon of choice for God and His angelic warriors. It was not "invented" or "discovered," it was *revealed*; "After [the LORD] drove the man out, he placed on the east side of the Garden of Eden cherubim and a flaming sword flashing back and forth to guard the way to the tree of life" (Gen. 3:24).

Warriors throughout the ages have recognized the visual similarities between the sword and the cross. Knights traditionally prayed with their sword hilts held out in front of them as the sign of the cross and as a reminder of what they were fighting for. While on the quest for the Holy Grail, Sir Percival sees the hilt of his sword in a moment of temptation and is reminded of the cross of Christ, thus narrowly escaping his downfall.

Given the sword's divine origin, its use in Biblical imagery, its employment by celestial warriors, and the obvious pictorial symbolism, it should be no wonder that nothing has stood longer as a weapon destined to advance all causes that are holy, just, and righteous. It is an implement of valor, truth, and purity, and its misuse carries a terrible curse (Mt. 26:52). It served for ages as a symbol of chivalry and honor, and continues to do so today in literature and fantasy culture.

A Weapon of Beauty

Because the sword is an object of such immense symbolic value, these weapons have often been crafted with exquisite skill. Gold and silver inlays and precious stones set into the hilt reflect the personal value that the possessor places on the sword. It isn't just a weapon; it is an expression of their identity and a mark of their heritage.

The amount of money and attention that we spend on something tells others (and ourselves) how much we value that object, activity, person, or idea. In the ancient and medieval world, warfare was a part of almost every man's life. Conflict with neighbors was continual, and it would be rare for a male to get through life without being pressed into military service at some point. The sword that was used and trusted in battle would become a treasured possession later in life, much the same way that a farmer values the tractor that served him well for many years or how the captain of a ship feels a personal attachment to the vessel. A warrior would be reminded of many tales of valor every time he looked at his old sword, and he would undoubtedly take good care of his weapon even after his years of service came to an end. Very likely, he would pass the sword on to his own son when the time came, adding further value to the treasured object because it now

> *"A sword, a spade, and a thought should never be allowed to rust."*
>
> ~James Stephens

acquired "heirloom" status.

So it's not hard to understand why a man would spend the time and money to embellish his sword with precious stones or metals. It's as though he poured a small portion of his spirit into the weapon; sword and warrior have been forged together in times of danger and tempered by the fires of courage. The man grows weak with age, brave deeds are forgotten, and the work of his hand passes away with the turning of a few years. But the sword retains its beauty; the gems still shine brightly, the blade still flashes brilliantly, and the edge remains just as sharp as ever. The sword represents that within himself which remains unchanged with the passage of time; his stout heart, his devotion to justice, and his noble character will never rust nor dull.

> *"Lay this unto your breast: Old friends, like old swords, still are trusted best."*
>
> *~John Webster*

When the world examines us, where does it see our time and treasures being spent? If Christ is the greatest part of our identity, shouldn't it be clearly displayed in our lives and homes? The Sword of the Spirit has been our trusted friend and weapon through all of

> *"We may be certain that whatever God has made prominent in His Word, He intended to be conspicuous in our lives."*
>
> *~Charles Spurgeon*

life's battles, so what kind of care does it receive from us? Do you polish it daily to keep it from rusting by beginning each morning in the Word? Do you meditate on Scripture always to keep the edge from growing dull and the tip blunt? Do you proudly display it in all its beauty to everyone you meet, or is it carelessly tossed in the corner and gathering dust? Will you teach your children of its inestimable worth so that they care for it just as much when you pass it on to them? The world will always be able to tell the quality of the warrior by the care with which he treats his weapon.

A Weapon of Value

A finely crafted sword is acquired only at a great expense. Sometimes the sword was purchased at a price of more than a year's wages. Many times a sword was only acquired because it was handed down from previous generations, the responsibility of ownership falling on one man at a time over hundreds of years. Other times a sword may have been obtained as a trophy or war spoils, and the price was that of blood or valor. Perhaps a man's bravery, loyalty, or other service was rewarded by a grateful lord through the gift of a well-made sword; or maybe the years of service were the price of obtaining that sword. However it is acquired, a sword represents considerable value to its owner.

Many times, young heroes are given a sword as a "rite-of-passage" or "coming-of-age." The sword represents their own maturity and the passage into adulthood. With it come the responsibilities of grown-up life; duty to a liege lord, protection of home and family, and defense of truth and justice. The loss or destruction of the sword is usually symbolic of the neglect or abuse of these responsibilities, and is often a direct result of such behavior. Young King Arthur claims his right to rule as king by drawing a magic sword from a stone and anvil, subsequently breaking the same sword by using it to exact revenge. He put his pride and anger before his duty as king, and the breaking of the sword represented his unworthiness to rule. The sword cannot be mended; but because he learns from his mistake, a new sword can be acquired – although it will come with a steep price and the opportunity for yet another foolish mistake.

Sometimes the hero has been impatiently anticipating the bestowal of the sword for years, anxious to move ahead in life and strike out on their own into the wild. Other times, the hero is reluctant to accept the sword. He doesn't want to leave the old life behind, and he knows that with the sword will come trouble and violence. The personality of the hero determines his reaction to this momentous occasion, and quite often there will be mixed feelings involved. In the Hero's Journey pattern, the hero is typically reluctant to take the sword because of his "unlikeliness" as a warrior. He may feel unqualified or unworthy of such a weapon. But a sword is just an object, and the best that it can do is to draw out the hidden abilities and character of the one who wields it.

The intrinsic value of fine swords makes these weapons treasured literary icons. A sword is rarely "just a sword" in stories and books; it will usually carry some kind of special significance to the hero, even if he doesn't realize it right away. As time goes on, the hero comes to realize what it is about himself that the sword represents, enabling him to live up to his full potential. His identity becomes actualized through the development of his own skill with the sword, and he begins to appreciate the heritage that has been passed down to him. Finally, the hero no longer feels unworthy of the sword or inadequate in the duties which it carries with it. This process is critical to the hero's realization of his identity, which is yet one more part of his training for whatever lies ahead. The sword will continue to remind him of who he is, where he has come from, and what he is fighting for.

> *"What students would learn in American schools above all is the religion of Jesus Christ."*
>
> *~George Washington*

Our Christian heritage is one of our most valuable assets, and it is being threatened like never before in the world today. How many faithful men and women did it take to pass down the Gospel truth to us? How many generations have given life and liberty to protect the fire of God's Word and to keep it burning? We have an *immensely* heavy responsibility on our shoulders; a responsibility to all those who have gone before us and wielded the Sword of the Gospel and then put it into our hands. Who wouldn't feel unworthy or inadequate, being handed this great task? What are the dire consequences of losing or breaking that sword – that chain of Christian heritage that has been preserved over the course of two millennia?

> *"I am afraid that the schools will prove the very gates of hell, unless they diligently labor in explaining the Holy Scriptures and engraving them in the heart of the youth."*
>
> *~Martin Luther*

But here we have the secular humanist philosophy – on our televisions, in our schools, all around us – telling young people to just throw away everything that has been preserved by our ancestors and forerunners so that we can "live for ourselves" or "be our own person." It is an age of rebellion, and the dreadful cost will likely be the loss of much that is good and wholesome in the name of "open-mindedness" and "free-thinking," the most tragic of which will be the Gospel truth. The world today is teaching young people (and old people, and everyone in between) not to believe anything that you've been told by parents, teachers, pastors, or especially old books. The irony is that *they are being "told" this – and believing it*! There was a time when parents, teachers, and pastors were looked at as pillars of wisdom. There was a time when "old books" were a fountain source of practical knowledge and truth, and the Bible was revered as sacred. But sadly, it is not today.

In every family line, there may be someone who fails to see the value of the sword. In fat and pursy times, it may sit on the closet shelf, buried in junk and forgotten. There may even be a prodigal fellow who trades it away, loses it, or breaks it through his own carelessness. But it is valuable all the same, because of what it is and what it has done for the family and the world in the past. And so it is with our own Christian heritage. It *must* be preserved at all costs; we must cherish it and teach our children why it is so valuable. We must never lose it or let harm come to it through abuse or neglect, because our lives and souls will one day depend upon it, as will those of our children and grandchildren. Do everything you can to instill this lesson in your children's hearts, and be sure that you are not the one who is responsible for losing such a priceless treasure.

A Weapon of Elegance

"It's your father's lightsaber. This is the weapon of a Jedi Knight. Not as clumsy or as random as a blaster, but a more elegant weapon for a more civilized age. For years, the Jedi were the guardians of peace and justice in the galaxy. Before the dark times..." ~Obi-Wan Kenobi in Star Wars, Episode IV

Swords are beautiful not just because of what they are and how they look, but also for how they are used. Swordplay is a form of art that requires graceful actions and fluid movements. Guns tend to be loud and unpredictable; anyone can pick one up and cause a great deal of damage very quickly. But a sword requires skill, training, and discipline. And it is that very discipline that teaches the user how a sword should and should not be used. It is not a weapon for cowards or lazy villains bent on revenge. It is a skill that requires years of training, purging the mind of rash behavior and hasty action.

> *"I do not love the bright sword for its sharpness, nor the arrow for its swiftness, nor the warrior for his glory. I love only that which they defend."*
>
> *~J.R.R. Tolkien*

There is a good reason why guns have come to represent death and destruction while swords represent such qualities as justice, courage, loyalty, and the like. Guns can certainly be used to effectively fight crime and keep the peace, but no one can deny the inherent grace and subtlety of a sword in the hands of an expert. The sword is a symbol of honor and chivalry from a time long before guns made it possible to deliver mass death and mayhem without any training whatsoever. There is something keenly tragic in the fact that swords have now been rendered obsolete. It reminds us that often "progress" comes at the price of losing some of the most important things in life.

Despite the decline in the sword's practical use in society, it is still seen as a symbol of all that we admire in a warrior. Perhaps the very reason there is so much fascination with fantasy and medieval life today is that we feel a sense of nostalgia for *something* – for whatever it is that was lost when the sword fell out of use after thousands of years. It represents the dream of a world that *once was*, and all of the good qualities that throve in that time. In an age of cowardice and uncertainty, the sword reminds us of a time when hearts were bold and brave deeds were commonplace. In an age of gray, muddy, amoral existentialism, it brings to mind a time when men fought for truth and purity, and evil was denounced for what it really is and driven out of the land. In an age of foolish litigation, broken legal systems, and unending bureaucracy, the sword reminds us of knights who were good and noble, who upheld the laws faithfully and executed justice swiftly and could always be trusted to protect the innocent. We put the sword and the gun side by side and look at the world

> *"And each man stands with his face in the light of his own drawn sword. Ready to do what a hero can."*
>
> ~*Elizabeth Barrett Browning*

that each one represents, and it's just about enough to make a person sick.

I know, I know; that isn't fair. Aren't we idealizing the past? Aren't we romanticizing history so that it literally becomes a fantasy that never really happened? Why, yes we are. That's one of the best

> *"Never mind searching for who you are. Search for the person you aspire to be."*
>
> *~Robert Brault*

things about fantasy. Why shouldn't we idealize and romanticize? Have we become so numb as a society that we are bound by heart-breaking realism in everything that we think and do? Who cares if our nostalgia is for a world that never existed – the point is to *crave* the things that know have been lost from our world, even if they were never where we thought they were in the first place! We should *long* for a society that values boldness and valor. We should *yearn* for a time when we will recognize what is good and denounce what is evil once again. We should *ache* for a world where the strong help the weak, and strength is seen merely as a means to defend the vulnerable.

> *"Nurture you mind with great thoughts; to believe in the heroic makes heroes."*
>
> *~Benjamin Disraeli*

I believe in the sword. I wholeheartedly promote any story today that reminds humanity of what it once was, or at least could have been, because these stories give me hope that such a time may one day come again. Right now, the sword lies in pieces, broken to bits by the bullets and bombs of today, a tragic symbol. But as long as we remember that the pieces are there, they might someday be re-forged and made whole once more. Men and women would stir up their hearts and find the noble qualities that long ago settled to the bottom and were forgotten. Honor and chivalry would revive, courage and valor would ignite, and the time of the sword would rise again.

It was a beautiful world back then, before the dark times… It is my heart's desire to return there.

Chapter VI
Elves, Fairies, and Other Sylvan Creatures: ...and They Woodland Where, Exactly?

About a thousand years ago, the cutting edge medical researchers of the time were working on discovering the source of airborne illnesses. What was it that caused otherwise healthy humans to suddenly contract terrible diseases? Optimism was high as one breakthrough led to another, and top notch medical experts from around Europe corresponded in the most aggressive concerted effort to root out and eliminate the cause of so much human suffering. After years of painstaking research and intensive laboratory testing, a consensus was finally reached among the academic elite: It was elves shooting invisible darts into unwary foot-travelers.

The "elf" has a rich history and tradition in literature. So how did these quaint little forest dwellers go from being suspected medieval biological terrorists, to building toys at the North Pole, to baking cookies in a tree, to battling the forces of darkness in Middle Earth? The process was long and convoluted, weaving pagan superstitions into the mix of contemporary Christian dogma on the loom of daily provincial life.

Elves, fairies, dryads, and other assorted magical forest dwellers were all products of pagan tribal beliefs in ancient Europe, much akin to the centaurs, harpies, and sirens of ancient Greek society. While sometimes good and sometimes bad and always mischievous, these "fey-folk" took the blame for many problems that were not properly understood by the people of the time. However, they were a perceived reality and became a part of daily life for many peasants, woodsmen, and merchants who had to travel through forests and along wilderness roads regularly.

So Christian missionaries come along and bring the Gospel to the people of northern Europe. Just imagine the monumental task of trying to explain mankind's fall into sin, the promise of a Messiah, the fulfillment of Old Testament prophecies in Christ, and everything in between – all the while battling not only a massive language barrier but also struggling with these pagan superstitions that are built into their framework of reality. I figure it went something like this:

> Peasant: "So, would ye say that the elves and fairies work for the Devil?"
>
> Missionary: "What elves and fairies?"
>
> Peasant: "The ones in the wood what keep shootin' us with them tiny disease-ridden arrows?"
>
> Missionary: "I…didn't see any elves or… Look, all of the diseases and problems in our lives are caused by sin."
>
> Peasant: "Ah, yes, I see it now. So the elves dip their arrows into a wee bottle o' sin before they shoot 'em into us."

Missionary: "No, no, there aren't any elves or fairies. Our world is cursed and fallen because…"

Peasant: "Well then who's shootin' all them tiny darts at us all the time? You can't 'spect us to believe that this Devil fellow is fast enough to go 'round doin' all that by himself, do ye?"

Missionary: "We don't get 'shot' with anything; we're *born* with sin already in us."

Peasant: "Ya mean to tell me those sneaky li'l pixies ha' found their way into the nurs'ry?! We'll hafta have ma' mix up some good mud and fill them holes what is lettin' in all the…"

Missionary: "Yeah, you know what? The elves and fairies work for the Devil."

After enough time went by, the "doctrine of elves" was simply accepted by the Church and incorporated into the local belief system, lumping them in with demons, imps, succubae, incubi, and the like.

Peasant: "Sir? A fairy's been botherin' me on me way to work ev'ry mornin', and I don't know what t' do."

Missionary: "A fairy? But I told you, there aren't any…"

Peasant: "This one's a partic'lary nasty lit'l blighter, but I think I know where he's been hidin'. See, there's this hollow log…"

Missionary: "Okay, okay, fine. Let me see... have you tried wearing a cross?"

Peasant: "I reckon that'd scare 'em off, but it don't seem all that practic'l, luggin' that big ole thing around every..."

Missionary: "No, no, no; a small one, that you could put on a chain around your neck and pull it out to ward off the fairy."

Peasant: "How's that gonna' scare off me fairy again, gov'?"

Missionary: "Well, the fairy works for the Devil, *remember*? So he will flee from any reminder of God's love for you."

Peasant: "Ah, yeah, I see it now. So I'll just take this and... hold on. What if I forget to take me cross one day?"

Missionary: "You could make the sign of the cross using your fingers."

Peasant: "I dunno... how about garlic or wolfs bane? I o'erheard Smitty Gunderson saying that works mighty well on..."

Missionary: "No, I think we'll stick to crosses. Or say the Lord's Prayer to show the fairy that you're a child of God."

Peasant: "Ah, right'o! Like a magic spell or somethin' to ward off the lit'l beastie."

Missionary: "Um, no, it isn't like that at all actually. Why don't you just pray and ask God to give you the strength and patience to bear with your unwanted visitor?"

Peasant: "Bangers! Does that really work?"

Missionary: (smiling) "It always does for me."

And so, the elf and his kinfolk were adopted into medieval Christian lore, effectively becoming accomplices of devils and demons and the source of all manner of illnesses and afflictions. For centuries afterward, elves and fairies were therefore seen as patently evil, being minions of Satan and workers of his infernal will. Rightly so, they were categorized with witches, goblins, spooks, and other remnants of the old pagan superstitions.

Over time, however, the fey have found their rightful place in the annals of fantasy fiction, being purely a construct of ancient imagination and legend lore. Their role has greatly shifted from being evil and mischievous, to being just mischievous, to now generally being good and mischievous. Fairies have gone from being ugly little bugs to beautiful expressions of tiny feminine grace; a side-effect of their inward reformation of character that reflects the same literary principle as is seen with witches and sorceresses. Elves have also undergone a paradigm shift, evolving from short, gruesome little men with hooked noses and hairy warts to the noble, agile, and attractive warriors of the woodlands.

The roles of elves, fairies, and fey folk in fantasy literature reflect certain aspects of humanity and the human condition. As we read and study these creatures in literature, we can learn something about ourselves and the people around us. These mythical races inhabit the lush forests and shaded glens of imaginary worlds, helping us to discover and recognize the most elusive aspects of human nature along our own journey through the forest of life.

> *"Each has its lesson; for our dreams in sooth, come they in shape of demons, gods, or elves, are allegories with deep hearts of truth that tell us solemn secrets of ourselves."*
>
> *~Henry Timrod*

Defenders of Nature

Part of the reason that the role of fey creatures in literature has undergone such a dramatic shift is undoubtedly due to the fact that our understanding of nature itself has changed drastically. In ancient and medieval times, nature was dark, mysterious, and threatening. They did not see it as a benevolent force; it was beyond the known and civilized world and represented all of the dangers and perils of the unknown. It symbolized the darkness of *human* nature as well – that wild and untamed part of our souls that would run from God and dance madly around bonfires at strange sylvan rituals. Nature was evil, and the denizens of darkness roamed the forests and meres, waiting to do Satan's bidding.

> *"One impulse from a vernal wood*
> *May teach you more of man,*
> *Of moral evil and of good,*
> *Than all the sages can."*
>
> ~William Wordsworth

We live in a different world today. Nature seems sadly quelled to most people in modern society. In truth, there are still huge expanses of very wild and dangerous wilderness in all parts of the world, but we are so far removed from them that they seem distant and unreal. A thousand years ago, the forces of nature were pressing in on all sides, and the people had to encounter its cruelty on a daily basis. But for us, nature is a romantic notion – we think of it as being peaceful, serene, and pure. Actually, I would say that both of these assessments are completely accurate, and it is this very dichotomy that makes nature such a great parallel to *human* nature.

> *"Man's heart away from nature becomes hard."*
>
> *~Standing Bear*

So today, we see elves and fairies as good, kind, and benevolent because we tend to be inclined to understand the world they inhabit as such. All of them are representatives of nature and protectors of the forests and woodlands. Through the literary lens of fantasy, this translates them into defenders of all that is pure, green, and fair. Forests are teeming with abundant life, and anything that protects that life becomes an obvious symbol of the forces of light and good. The ancient world viewed the forests as dark and sinister; we view them as soft and gentle, possessing a more natural light than the piercing fluorescent lamps of the modern world. Long ago, the elves and other inhabitants of the woods were seen as lurking about in the shadows, dwelling in darkness and solitude; today, we see these creatures as shy and aloof, withdrawn from the stench and filth of the human world and living a subtle and understated existence in the treetops of sylvan sanctuaries.

> *"God writes the Gospel not in the Bible alone, but also on trees, and in the flowers and clouds and stars."*
>
> *~Martin Luther*

God created nature to be "very good," and the curse of sin has given even the forests of our world a taint of evil. Both light and darkness reside within their shadowy confines. Like magic, or swords, or any other device used in fantasy fiction, forests are not inherently good or bad. Many times, the hero must travel through an "evil forest" or a "cursed woods," and in these places he will not find the pure-hearted elves and fairies that protect the wholesome woods. If they do inhabit these "dark forests," they are usually a corrupt or perverted race that either migrated to the evil woods because of their own wicked inclinations or they have been warped and mutated by the dark forces present in the forest. On rare occasions, the hero may find a good elf or fairy in the dark forest, but only because that creature is there to assist him or to fight whatever evil lurks there – it would never choose to live in such a place.

We can learn something from these fey creatures. If we choose to live in darkness, our hearts become blackened and corrupted, mutating every aspect of our characters until we seem to "fit right in" with our evil surroundings. Those who are already black at heart seek out the places of darkness and eternally dwell therein. Those who are good and wholesome at heart avoid living in darkness; they flee from it and stay far away, lest they become infected with its evil taint. Occasionally, a pure heart will need to plunge into the dark places of this world in order to rescue another, or to combat and contain the evil that is hidden there, but it cannot endure living in such an awful place.

> *"I go to nature to be soothed and healed, and to have my senses put in order."*
>
> ~*John Burroughs*

Seek out the gentle forests. Whenever your journey leads you through one, find rest and renewal in the shade of its whispering branches. If you encounter the elusive residents of such places, accept their counsel and their aid, and learn whatever wisdom they may have to offer. For all too soon, your path will lead through yet another cursed woods, and you will need all your strength to resist its darkness and fend off its wicked inhabitants.

Learn to recognize and align yourself with the defenders of the woodland realms. While some may see them as aloof or even cowardly in their refusal to leave the protective confines of their trees, they are providing an invaluable service in preserving the wholesome, lush forests of our world. We *need* lush, leafy refuges wherein we can always find rest and protection, and it is their strength that keeps these green havens safe. Sylvan creatures fall into a natural symbiotic relationship with their wooded surroundings; their "magic" thrives in the forest realms as they draw their power from the peaceful world, and they vigilantly secure the forest borders from fire, axes, and any other invasive evils that would infect the trees with dark diseases.

In our world, warriors of the faith who fight on the front lines need a place to which they can retreat from time to time. Thankfully, there are other warriors who remain behind and ensure that there will always be a peaceful locale where others can rest and recuperate. Christians who are engaged in mission work or involved in political or legal struggles on behalf of the faith community need to be able to have periods of "sabbatical" with stable home congregations, Christian communities, and supportive families. While there may be a temptation to become frustrated and believe that what they are doing is somehow more important, they must also recognize the vital role that the Christians behind them play in preserving a strong foundation for the faith. How many times would they be able to continue to go forth into battle against the forces of darkness without the rest and renewal that they continually receive from the "peaceful forests" in their lives? How could these sanctuaries of light continue to exist without faithful warriors garrisoned within to defend against apathy, hypocrisy, or even heresy? How could the battle continue without the resources that flow from the "woodlands" and the

> *"Here stands the font before our eyes, telling how God has received us. The altar recalls Christ's sacrifice and what His Supper here gives us. Here sound the Scriptures that proclaim Christ yesterday, today, the same, and evermore our Redeemer."*
>
> *~Nikolai Fredrik Severin Grundtvig: Built on the Rock*

new warriors that are constantly being trained there? Any wise warrior will not only quickly recognize how invaluable these "forests of the faith" are to all of us, but they will also be inspired to fight even more fiercely on the "front lines" in order to protect the canopy of shelter behind them.

A Touch of Magic: Creatures of Grace and Beauty

Chapters two and three talked about "magic" being analogous with any kind of power or special ability in our world; wisdom, artistic talent, charisma, leadership, etc. Those who wield magic have a particularly heavy burden of responsibility to use their abilities in a responsible manner. They also undergo a great deal of temptation to abuse their powers, using them for selfish reasons, personal gain, or destructive purposes. Wizards, sorceresses, necromancers, and witches all represent different kinds of people in our world. The kind of magic they possess – and more importantly how they *use* that magic – determines which groups of real world people are represented by their character archetype.

Elves, fairies, nymphs, dryads, unicorns, and all other sylvan or fey creatures are magical by nature. It flows through them and is a part of their very being. Sometimes it is willfully manifested in much the

> *"If one way be better than another, that you may be sure is nature's way."*
>
> *~Aristotle*

same way that a wizard or sorceress would use their magic; but often it is simply a constant, subtle force that gives them beauty, stealth, longevity, wisdom, agility, or any other trait that goes just a little beyond what is humanly possible for that characteristic. Because they are more closely connected with that part of nature that has been untainted by the curse of evil, their uncanny abilities surpass what is natural for mortals.

Just as human magic users represent different types of people in our world, magical sylvan creatures demonstrate the good and pure aspects of humanity. The taint of sin can cause even the noblest of intentions to become warped and perverted in our human weakness, eventually advancing the cause of the Devil more than that of the God we set out to serve. In order for human beings to really serve God, we need some power beyond our own. We are too weak and sinful to do any good work by our own reason or willpower. But the superhuman strength that comes from the Holy Spirit enables us to become the hands of the Living God, working to glorify Him on this earth and to serve our neighbors.

> *"Great things are done when men and mountains meet. This is not done by jostling in the street."*
>
> ~William Blake

In a sense, all Christians are elves. Mankind has been separated from God through Adam's fall into sin. We became dead in our trespasses and all that was good and pure within our hearts withered and died in the process. But immediately after the fall, God provided new life through the promise of a Savior (Gen. 3:15). Jesus Christ, the mediator between God and man, has restored the "nature" that God intended at the world's creation. Those who believe in Him are once again connected with the good and pure aspects of humanity through the Holy Spirit. To be sure, we must still daily "drown" our old sinful nature through remembering our baptism in repentance. But as we live in the lush, magical forests of God's grace and feed on the mystical fruit of His Word, we gradually become more and more "sylvan." In time, there are recognizable differences; not pointy ears or gossamer wings, but hearts that live for others and for God instead of for self alone. The Christian life flows with "magic" as we are empowered to perform feats of kindness, compassion, bravery, and selflessness that would not be humanly possible without the grace of God that courses through our veins. The Christian becomes a new creation, a different breed, a whole separate race.

It is true that good works are impossible without God. The fruits of the Spirit do not grow on withered fig trees or poisonous thorn bushes. So how is it that unbelievers can sometimes exhibit sudden bursts of Godly behavior? This book itself utilizes some quotes by individuals who openly rejected God. Yet even those who have no faith in the God who made them or the Savior who died for them can still unwittingly serve Him. However, this is still only possible through the influence of our good and merciful God and by His grace and power.

God's power cannot be contained within the green forests of Christian communities and churches, but instead flows outward into the surrounding wastelands where it encounters and quells the evil that resides there. Although many people sincerely believe that they are performing kind, generous, or otherwise noble deeds by their own power, the truth is that

> *"If he have faith, the believer cannot be restrained. He betrays himself. He breaks out. He confesses and teaches this Gospel to the people at the risk of life itself."*
>
> *~Martin Luther*

God is the root and source of everything good and pure in this world. Perhaps certain qualities or beliefs were instilled into this person by a distant relative or ancestor, by a teacher or friend, or even by a brief encounter with a stranger who made an impact on them. It is possible that even *that* person didn't fully realize why they valued that particular characteristic, but passed it on to others nonetheless because of their profound conviction of its essential "rightness." And every human being has trace remnants of the creatures God made us to be; His will is imprinted on our hearts in the form of a conscience that accuses us when we rebel and go astray.

There may be many people in this world who do not care about God, but God still cares deeply about them. His power works in wonderful and mysterious ways to produce good deeds from even the most unlikely hands, and it often works even more miraculously to produce faith in the most unlikely hearts. God's children may flee from His presence and turn their backs on Him, but they are still His creation and He loved them enough to give His only Son for them. When Christians grumble and complain about "good things happening to bad people," they should instead be reminded that those "bad people" are the ones most in need of God's merciful hand in their lives. They should rejoice that God "causes his sun to rise on the evil and the good, and sends rain on the righteous and the unrighteous" (Matt. 5:45).

There are no more graceful creatures in fantasy literature than elves, fairies, and the entire sylvan host. The "magic" of God's grace is what gives Christians their beauty, their spiritual agility, their wisdom, their kindness, and all the other supernatural powers that they possess. So what are we to do with these powers? Do we hide in our verdant woods, merrily living out our days frolicking under the green canopy of the Gospel? Or do God's sylvan creatures ally themselves with the beleaguered men of this world, risking all to drive back the forces of darkness that have beset them? While it may be tempting to retreat with Christian friends and families deep within the forests and ignore the spiritual slaughter all around us in the world, we know that mankind cannot and must not stand alone. We venture forth into the parched, burning wastes of the secular world – not to *combat* the people living there, but to aid and assist them. There, our powers will be put to good use for the healing and restoration of a wounded and stricken people. Our silver arrows will fly whistling over their heads to pierce the ranks of Satan's army, striking down his lies, his torments, and his accusations. We seek not the thanks of men, only their salvation. We serve the God who made us, saved us, and preserves us; we see His sorrow over their suffering and destruction, and we are moved to fight valiantly for pity's sake.

Where the elven host marches, there is hope in the face of death and despair. Now let us move swiftly and silently, that the enemy may be taken unawares and shocked by our ferocity. May our barrage of arrows batter Satan's ranks and drive him to retreat in shame. Then, the forests will spread, the wastelands will become green and verdant once again, and all the people of this land will enjoy peace and the blessings of our great Lord. Now is the time to raise the sylvan banners and sound the trumpet of the woodland realms.

Chapter VII
Orcs, Goblins, and Everyday Challenges

Every genre in literature has one type of character that stands for the universal "bad guy." This character archetype isn't always the main villain or protagonist, but will pop up recurrently to throw the proverbial monkey wrench into the plans of the hero. In old westerns, it was the Indians. In action or super-hero fiction, it's the army of ever-present street thugs. Indiana Jones battles his way past dozens of Nazi scumbags, and Luke Skywalker and his entourage plow through hordes of supposedly "elite" storm troopers as they locate and neutralize the *real* threat to humanity.

In fantasy fiction, no creature better fits this mold than the goblin. While there are a few notable exceptions, goblins are the archetypical enemy of nearly every fledgling warrior and wizard in the fantasy realm. They pose an ever-present threat and often significantly complicate the mission of the hero, slowing progress and exposing him to further dangers. Tolkien, who is rightly regarded by many as the father of modern fantasy fiction, gives a wonderful description of goblins in *The Hobbit*, and many of the characteristics he outlines have endured in goblinhood for over seven decades:

"Now goblins are cruel, wicked, and bad-hearted. They make no beautiful things, but they make many clever ones. They can tunnel and mine as well as any but the most skilled dwarves, when they take

the trouble, though they are usually untidy and dirty. Hammers, axes, swords, daggers, pickaxes, tongs, and also instruments of torture, they make very well, or get other people to make to their design, prisoners and slaves that have to work till they die for want of air and light. It is not unlikely that they invented some of the machines that have since troubled the world, especially the ingenious devices for killing large numbers of people at once, for wheels and engines and explosions always delighted them, and also not working with their own hands more than they could help; but in those days and those wild parts they had not advanced (as it is called) so far. They did not hate dwarves especially, no more than they hated everybody and everything, and particularly the orderly and prosperous... and anyway goblins don't care who they catch, as long as it is done smart and secret, and the prisoners are not able to defend themselves."

As you can see, goblin paragons are the antithesis of the sylvan creature. Their dominant characteristics are violence, deception, laziness, greed, lawlessness, cruelty, cowardice, and a disposition generally inclined toward destruction and mayhem. If it's beautiful, smash it; if it's pure, defile it; if it's green or good or in any way wholesome, burn it. They are either aligned with the dark powers that threaten to consume the hero's world or owe allegiance to no one in particular, acting in a way that promotes chaos and anarchy. Either way, they are a dangerous and unpredictable foe that is often overlooked and whose threat is always underestimated.

The Elf and the Goblin: The foul offspring of twisted virtue

"Goblins are cruel, wicked, and bad-hearted"

Goblins simply cannot be trusted under any circumstances. Their nature is so vile and wicked that virtue is actually a racial impossibility for them. They are everything that the elves detest, and the two will be eternally at warfare with each other because their ideologies cannot peacefully coexist. In fact, Tolkien explains in *The Lord of the Rings* trilogy that the orcs (or goblins) were actually elves once, and that their perverse nature is the result of their true natures being warped and twisted by the "dark powers" until they became the despicable creatures they are now.

It should be no wonder that such enmity exists between elves and goblins; though to be fair, while the goblins particularly despise the elves, they have a great deal of enmity towards *anything* good, peaceful, or otherwise decent. For the elves' part, we know that it is especially easy to be quite scornful or even fearful toward those things which we have overcome in the past and no longer wish to recollect. Perhaps the only thing more hateful to us is the image of what we might become if the

> *"A beast does not know that he is a beast, and the nearer a man gets to being a beast, the less he knows it."*
>
> ~George MacDonald

"dark powers" were to take hold of *our* hearts and wills and warp them into a grotesque distortion of our former selves.

How can such evil originate with something so good and pure? As with many other things in our world – food, wealth, technology, pharmaceuticals – objects and pursuits that were designed to be good and helpful can be misused and abused in a way that renders them wicked and harmful. It isn't difficult to see how Tolkien's goblins represent all of the generous gifts that God bestows upon His children that are then corrupted and inverted to serve evil intentions. And unfortunately, the twisted versions of these gifts are not always as distinguishable to us as would be a goblin hiding among elves.

Goblins throughout fantasy fiction have become a symbol of evil and cruelty, something to be actively hunted and destroyed by noble warriors on the quest. In the *Harry Potter* series, Rowling portrays goblins as maintaining a fragile coexistence with the wizards. Even so, there is a steady current of enmity between these two groups, and many of the undesirable characteristics of Tolkien's goblins remain firmly planted in the hearts of Griphook and his compatriots. Countless other books, games, and movies have portrayed goblins as the universal antagonists; a tide of hostility toward the hero, nature, and the world in general.

> *"Cruelty, like every other vice, requires no motive outside itself; it only requires opportunity."*
>
> *~George Eliot*

The Dwarf and the Goblin: Beauty vs. Utility

"They make no beautiful things, but they make many clever ones. They can tunnel and mine as well as any but the most skilled dwarves, when they take the trouble, though they are usually untidy and dirty. Hammers, axes, swords, daggers, pickaxes, tongs, and also instruments of torture, they make very well, or get other people to make to their design, prisoners and slaves that have to work till they die for want of air and light. It is not unlikely that they invented some of the machines that have since troubled the world, especially the ingenious devices for killing large numbers of people at once, for wheels and engines and explosions always delighted them, and also not working with their own hands more than they could help; but in those days and those wild parts they had not advanced (as it is called) so far."

The elven race is not the only fantasy species that is weirdly paralleled by goblins. Dwarves also bear some strange similarities to goblins, albeit these likenesses are once again corrupted by the goblins' evil nature. There is no race in fantasy more famed for craftsmanship than the dwarves, and their skill in creating weapons, armor, fine jewelry, musical instruments, toys, and many other oddities is unparalleled. They obtain great wealth by means of their trade, both in the export of finished goods and also from the tutelage of apprentices who come from far and wide to work under them and learn even a bit of dwarven smith-lore. Great friendships and alliances are forged with neighboring kings through the gifting of finely crafted objects which become great family heirlooms and treasured possessions (the loss of which, incidentally and ironically, often leads to war...). Dwarven weapons and armor constitute some of the most sought-after relics in the annals of fantasy fiction, often glittering with sparkling gems of unsurpassed clarity that betray the secret of the item's origin. Whatever dwarves make, you can be sure that the quality, craftsmanship, and beauty of the finished product will clearly indicate to all that it came from the forges of the dwarven smiths.

Dwarves also take pride in their ability to craft stone tunnels and dwellings. They carve great bastions out of solid mountains, sculpting magnificent cities and great halls underground and mining in shafts that reflect the precision and aesthetic discipline of the dwarven race. Their mines and cities are clean, well-maintained, and possess balance and symmetry. While functioning with meticulous exactitude, their halls and tunnels are also adorned with intricate carvings and detailed masonry. In mining and carving, as well as in forging, the pride of their race is reflected in the work of their hands.

> *"Whatever you do, work at it with all your heart, as working for the Lord, not for men."*
>
> *~Colossians 3:23*

What, then, of their goblin counterparts? If necessity is the mother of invention, then the malice and cruelty of the goblins drives them to create tools of torture and destruction. Although generally slow-witted (often comically so), their "need" to inflict pain and devastation motivates even these unintelligent creatures to develop and produce cleverly crafted instruments and mechanical devices. Their search for raw materials and the expansion of their territory drives them to hastily extend their network of tunnels with a speed that rivals even that of the dwarves. However, their tunnels are crude, dirty, and winding, lacking the careful planning and precision of the dwarves. Dwarves do everything to the best of their abilities; something that is a noble and admirable trait. Goblins do everything with as little effort as possible, and often try to avoid doing it themselves if given an option.

Like the dwarves, goblins take pride in the work of their hands; however, they consider this work to be plundering, pillaging, and causing widespread misery rather than crafting fine workmanship that will endure for generations to come. While the dwarves see their quintessential task as being to create, beautify, and restore, goblins believe the goal of their existence is to destroy, kill, and torment. Dwarves represent the pinnacle of orderly society, striving to civilize the wild and improve living conditions for all. Goblins strive to undo whatever useful or beautiful things society constructs, and the only things that are "useful" to them are those objects which help them achieve that end. The dichotomy is one of order and prosperity versus chaos and deterioration, and the same set of skills and abilities can be employed toward either cause.

The enmity between dwarves and goblins – whether caused by their similarities or their differences – provides an important balance in the fantasy world. As Vita Sackville-West points out,

"It is very necessary to have markers of beauty left in a world seemingly bent on making the most evil ugliness." Though the beautiful dwarven relics may be stolen, horded and despoiled by the goblins, what would the world be like without their continued production? Though the magnificent dwarven halls may become infested with goblin invaders and befouled with their filth and stink, would we dare to suggest that the noble dwarves abandon the task of creating and maintaining such wondrous bastions? What would become of the world without the stout dwarven defenders to encounter the goblin hordes in underground battles, standing between order and turmoil, beauty and oblivion?

Of course we know that the dwarven race is vital to the survival of all that is good and pure in the fantasy world. It is in the very goodness and purity of these fictional realms that we find what we long for in our world. We know that it isn't *real*, but it reflects the truth of necessary warfare against a continual

> "The only thing necessary for the triumph of evil is for good men to do nothing."
>
> ~Edmund Burke

onslaught of ugly cruelty and heartless practicality that occurs in *our* world every day. It reminds us of our duty as Christians, and inspires us to stand between the evil of the world and the generation that will come after us. What would happen without the authors and artists who declare the beauty of these immortal truths to all who are willing to cast more than a perfunctory glance at God's eternal monuments?

Yes, I believe Christian authors are well represented by the dwarven archetype, as are other artists, teachers, pastors, or anyone who directs mankind to God's universal truths. It must be frustrating – to see the beautiful works of one's hands taken by vicious foes who misuse them; to see them fall into disrepair and ruin as they are kept hoarded and hidden away from the world. But they must not give up. It is essential that they continue to carve, chisel, and forge in their mountain caves, turning out the objects of beauty that protect lives while also calling to mind the power of the One who gives order and light. I agree with Emerson: "Everything in creation has its appointed painter or poet and remains in bondage like the princess in the fairy tale 'til its appropriate liberator comes to set it free." Through sin, the Devil has taken captive many of the profound and wonderful ways that we are reminded of God's truth in this world. We are God's hands here on earth to release the sculptures from their prisons of stone and hold them up for all to see their beauty and splendor.

> *"Beauty is the mark God sets on virtue. Every natural action is graceful; every heroic act is also decent, and causes the place and the bystanders to shine."*
>
> *~Ralph Waldo Emerson*

Find and release beauty wherever possible. Not every fantasy book mentions God by name, but nearly all of them exalt the fruits of His Spirit. Use these opportunities to instill values such as courage, compassion, and integrity in your own heart and the hearts of those whom God has entrusted to your care. Help them to understand why these characteristics are God-pleasing, and foster in them a burning desire to stand firmly for their Lord and King. In fantasy fiction, those things and people that are inherently good also have a lasting beauty; a paradigm that helps readers to differentiate between good and evil in the real world. Dwarves are the craftsmen and caretakers of the beautiful, and we are called to be such in our own positions in life.

There is a certain danger in mankind's tendency to ignore the beautiful for the sake of the practical. The goblins tunnel in order to get somewhere; the dwarves tunnel in order to get somewhere as well, but will not miss the opportunity of creating something grand in the process. Therefore, the dwarf is forced to apply the whole of his skill and his art to the task at hand, while the goblin works haphazardly and with little real effort or focus. Art and beauty are noble pursuits; they not only inspire and revive the human spirit, but they also develop and sharpen Godly characteristics in the artist. In reality, the product or result the craftsman puts forth is a testament to his or her own inner character. As Edwin Teale puts it, "The difference between *utility* and *utility plus beauty* is the difference between telephone wires and the spider web."

The noble character of the dwarven race drives them to contribute a sense of beauty, grandeur, or elegance to *everything* they create. But many of the things they create are made *only* for the sake of beauty. I have personally encountered in the world today a growing sense that anything created solely for the purpose of beauty is a worthless endeavor, a waste of precious time. This is goblin thinking. Dwarves create golden harps studded with glittering gems only for the sake of producing exquisite music. Of what value is that to a goblin? Screams of pain are the only sounds that they enjoy – their world and mindset are foreign to the thinking of the wholesome races of dwarves, elves, and even men. When we criticize members of society who are dedicated to the arts, we might as well ask God, "What good is a sunset?" James Russell Lowell puts it this way: "The question of common sense is always what is it good for? – a question which would abolish the rose and be answered triumphantly by the cabbage."

Goblins not only have a profound lack of appreciation for beauty, they are downright hostile toward it. They seek to repress and annihilate it wherever they can, in whomever they can. There is a natural enmity between them and the inherent beauty of nature. They live in a habitation that lacks fresh air, sunlight, and green foliage – three elements that are universally recognized as necessary

> *"Every genuine work of art has as much reason for being as the earth and the sun."*
>
> *~Ralph Waldo Emerson*

commodities of God's creation. Tolkien notes that goblins' prisoners "have to work till they die for want of air and light." Without the beauty of nature, or any beauty for that matter, the human spirit grows weaker and is eventually crushed by the evil that surrounds them. Lewis Mumford addresses the phenomenon when he says, "A day spent without the sight or sound of beauty, the contemplation of mystery, or the search for truth or perfection is a poverty-stricken day; and a succession of such days is fatal to human life."

Sadly, Mumford describes exactly the direction that our society is headed. In schools, art and music programs are dropped in favor of more "practical" pursuits so that the upcoming generation of workers will constitute a more productive work force than that of our nation's neighbors (doesn't that absolutely *reek* of goblin philosophy? – and the kicker is that it doesn't even seem to be working...). In English classes, many schools and individual teachers have given up trying to help young people understand and appreciate beautiful literature and poetry, opting instead to teach them "survival skills" that will get them through trade school and help them operate in an office environment. History is taught as a conglomeration of essential facts rather than the collective wisdom of the human experience over the ages. Students are taught that they must excel in mathematics and science so that they can become productive citizens and earn the necessary income to support a lifestyle of empty materialism, not because they are to use their skills and knowledge to the best of their ability to God's glory and in service to their fellow man. This general educational philosophy engenders an ability to *exist*; God's will for us is to *live*, and learning to appreciate the beauty of His world enables us to do so fully.

Goblins vs. Men: Craftiness and deception in place of valor

> *"In every man's heart there is a secret nerve that answers to the vibrations of beauty."*
>
> *~Christopher Morley*

"...anyway goblins don't care who they catch, as long as it is done smart and secret, and the prisoners are not able to defend themselves."

Disgusting. Truly shameful. King Arthur would never have stood for it.

Valor is one of the pillars of chivalry, and noble men in all time periods and in all literary genres uphold it as an essential characteristic. It doesn't mean courage alone, but also worthiness, respectability, goodness. It should come as no surprise, then, that goblins lack valor completely.

A noble knight is expected to act with valor at all times. This meant that he would never, under any circumstances, attack a foe using trickery or deceit. Furthermore, he would never attack an unarmed or helpless opponent. If the enemy was outnumbered or somehow handicapped, he would make concessions to "even the odds." Perhaps this would mean lending his opponent a sword or armor, dismounting from his horse so they were on equal ground, or encountering a lone opponent in single combat instead of *en masse* with his companions. Some people would say, "well, that's just stupid." There, again, is goblin thinking – "practicality" and "utility" are at the heart of that logic. Beauty and honor dictate to the knight that his own integrity and character are of the utmost importance; perhaps even more important than achieving whatever goal lies before him.

Honor means nothing to a goblin, so he will gladly sacrifice it in order to subdue his opponent with minimal effort and minimal risk. It is a shallow, empty victory; but the ends must justify the means. Yet when men sacrifice *their* honor for *any* reason, they have lost an essential part of their being. In

> *"Chivalry!---why, maiden, she is the nurse of pure and high affection---the stay of the oppressed, the redresser of grievances, the curb of the power of the tyrant ---Nobility were but an empty name without her, and liberty finds the best protection in her lance and her sword."*
>
> *~Sir Walter Scott*

the chivalric code, the purpose of the quest was to test and refine the knight. Whatever other superficial "goal" was placed before them – finding a sacred object, traveling to a distant location, capturing a certain enemy – was purely a means by which this personal development was to occur. When the knight puts *anything* before virtue, they have automatically failed the quest.

> "You are a man, my boy, when you realize that every woman is entitled to your admiration, every child to your protection and every animal to the gentle stroke of your hand."
>
> ~Robert Brault

In the Arthur legend, King Pellinore fails in just such a way. He is commissioned with the task of finding a certain young noblewoman and bringing her to Camelot. Along the way, he encounters a young woman whose lover is wounded and dying. She pleads with him to help her, but he is so focused with completing his task that he rides on, thinking he hasn't the time. He ignores his duty to show mercy, put the service of women foremost, and aid all those in distress. Although he finds the noblewoman as tasked, he misses the point of the quest and ultimately fails as a knight; a fact that is reinforced by his eternal pursuit of the elusive "questing beast" which he is destined never to kill.

Not that this would mean much to a goblin. Perhaps there are a few goblins out there right now, saying to themselves, "So what? He did what Arthur told him to do, and that's all that matters." But noble knights believe that the *way* you do something is just as important as success or failure, perhaps even more so. Goblins will use any means possible to achieve their goals – which are never lofty or honorable – and consider it an outright *dishonor* to act with courage, compassion, or any kind of fairness.

In fantasy fiction, noble knights are the paragon of the world of men. They represent the virtues and characteristics that are desirable in all mankind and the traits that we are most noted for in literature. As a man loses his honor, his dignity, his loyalty, and so forth, his motives for heroic action gradually change until he becomes first a mercenary, and finally a villain. It is the manner in which the man acts and the motivation for this action that separates the men from the goblins. In the end, goblins have no good nature, no virtue, and no trace of the purity of the Creator in them. Sylvan creatures abound in grace and beauty. Men fall somewhere in between, having both the capacity to follow their King's will closely and act with honor, as well as the tendency to unscrupulously perform wicked deeds wrought from craftiness and deception. The "quest" is the opportunity for them to daily choose their path and exercise true valor in the face of danger.

The Weakling Goblin and the Danger of the "Cannon Fodder" Philosophy

True, goblins are pretty much universally portrayed as vile, wicked, sleazy, disgusting little vermin that serve little purpose other than target practice for heroes-in-training. Normal goblins, by themselves, are almost never portrayed as a serious threat to the heroes, but rather a nuisance; pesky intruders that complicate their plans and expose them to further danger. So the "goblin" archetype becomes symbolic for those "everyday" trials that we face in life – disgusting little spiritual pests like minor illnesses, flat tires, and difficult coworkers (or at least the thoughts and feelings that we permit ourselves in their presence). Goblins plague us in the form of small temptations or "minor" sins, things that we don't pay a lot of attention to because they just don't seem like all that big of a threat to our spiritual well-being. A warrior like me ought to be able to hack his way through this crowd of puny, pesky goblins with no problem, right?

Well, the goblins on our journey *can* pose a serious threat to us, and often it is for the very reason that we don't take them seriously. Even though goblins might be weak, clumsy, and stupid, they are still always armed with a deadly weapon, a nasty disposition, and a certain penchant for stealth and deception. They have a way of sneaking up on you in dark tunnels and setting traps for you when you least expect it. Before you know it, the little buggers are all over you, pulling you down and tying you up. Pretty soon, you're being dragged off into their dungeons, helpless and ashamed.

Yes, *every* goblin presents a threat to the safety and well-being of the hero. This is especially true when that hero is injured, impaired, unsuspecting, or otherwise helpless. When our faith has been weakened by all the tribulations life has to offer, even "minor" sins or temptations can be spiritually devastating. The fact that "I *should* be able to handle this" makes it even worse; I start to rely on my own strength to get me through difficult times, and then I despair and lose faith when I don't have it in me.

Goblins also have a knack for attacking us at the worst possible moments. A problem that would normally be only a minor annoyance can easily become a major setback to our ministry if it happens at the wrong time. The printer quits working just when you really needed it, the car breaks down right when you're short on cash, or you catch a cold just before a big presentation for work. All of the sudden these "little" problems make us do and say things we normally wouldn't, and we are left with a broken reputation, injured relationships, and a weakened faith.

> *"Seeing that a Pilot steers the ship in which we sail, who will never allow us to perish even in the midst of shipwrecks, there is no reason why our minds should be overwhelmed with fear and overcome with weariness."*
>
> ~*John Calvin*

Despite their reputation as hopeless wastrels, there is one way in which goblins occasionally pose a major threat to the well-being of heroes and their worlds. When goblins organize themselves and attack in unison, their sheer numbers present a force that can overwhelm even the mightiest armies. It doesn't happen often, but when it does, the world is faced with complete and utter destruction. Goblins are easily aligned with other evil factions, and the strength of their numbers provides the bulk of any wicked leader's fighting force.

Although we can usually fight off the kind of problem that goblins represent in our lives, we can easily be crushed when beset by a multitude of such woes. Suddenly, it feels as if the whole world is against us and *everything* is going wrong all at once. Wave after wave slams into us as problems pile up on top of each other, and we can hardly breathe as we try to meet each new challenge without fully resolving the once before. These are the times when the goblins in our lives pose a particularly serious threat, and we need the help of outside forces before we become overwhelmed.

> *"See round Your ark the hungry billows curling; See how Your foes their banners are unfurling and with great spite their fiery darts are hurling, O Lord, preserve us."*
>
> *"Lord, be our light when worldly darkness veils us; Lord, be our shield when earthly armor fails us; And in the day when hell itself assails us, Grant us Your peace, Lord."*
>
> ~Matthaus Appelles von Lowenstern: Lord of Our Life

Thankfully, help is never too far away. And thankfully, goblins are particularly cowardly creatures that will flee and disperse at the first sign of defeat. Send out a distress call to the Christian warriors around you. Call on the sylvan creatures of the forest to come quickly to your aid. Cry out to the King and cast your cares upon Him. Soon, the clouds will break and the piercing brilliance will dazzle the goblin ranks. God will send friends, allies, and powerful denizens of light to aid you in your fight. The ranks of goblins will be rent asunder, the charge will burst through their lines, and they will be driven off and scattered from your presence. Trust not in your own power, but sound a general call-to-arms for all those who stand against the darkness. Though countless foes beset you, God will grant you victory for His name's sake.

We Have Nothing to Fear but... Hobgoblins, Bugbears, and Boogeymen

In modern fantasy books, games, and movies, hobgoblins are typically regarded as upgraded versions of goblins (bigger, stronger, smarter, etc.), though an exhaustive search of European folklore would probably reveal them to be quite the opposite. Outside of the fantasy world, however, modern culture understands the term "hobgoblin" as the cause of some imagined fear. It could be an object, condition, or event that preys on our fear and sense of foreboding, although in reality there is very little (if any) actual danger posed by the "hobgoblin" in question. Since the literal creature was originally understood to be a small, impish being that played tricks on people but was generally considered harmless, it's easy to see how this interpretation evolved.

If we could put on a pair of "hobgoblin-vision glasses," we would see little hairy critters clinging to backs of everyone we meet. Some people constantly imagine that they will fail at whatever endeavor they have currently undertaken. Others suffer from a perpetual fear of rejection or abandonment by a significant other. And countless individuals imagine that all sorts of critical talk about them is occurring behind their backs at work, school, or in their social circles. The tragic irony is that these unjustified fears often lead to the very event that the person is afraid of becoming a reality (much like the "self-fulfilling prophecy" in Chapter I).

Sadly, people pay little attention to the "goblins" their lives – everyday challenges that normally pose only a minor threat but could prove extremely harmful under the right circumstances or in large numbers – and neglect even a healthy level of fear in regard to them. On the other hand, they harbor obsessive fears over their "hobgoblins" – imagined threats that actually pose very little danger except that which arises out of their own unreasonable terror – and turn mere phantoms into corporeal monsters with razor sharp fangs and claws. As President Franklin Roosevelt said, "The only thing we have to fear is fear itself – nameless, unreasoning, unjustified terror."

> *"Feed your faith and your fears will starve to death."*
>
> *~Anonymous*

As if hobgoblins weren't enough to paralyze us with unfounded terrors and keep us from productive action, we also have to deal with bugbears. Bugbears are related to hobgoblins, but are generally visualized as large, hairy, grotesque monsters. They are the embodiment of all the things that *others* tell us in order to make us do or not do something. They are the invented source of consequences for not going with the flow, keeping up with the Joneses, or caving to some other social pressure.

A mother in England might tell her child not to go into the forest because "the bugbears will get you!" While there may be plenty of real physical threats within the forest (drowning, falling, getting lost, etc.), it is the bugbear that actually accomplishes the desired result. The mother understands full well that the gentle, rolling brook holds no special terror for her child, even though it presents a constant danger with its icy waters, slippery rocks and deep pools. But the child can visualize clearly and vividly the crazed eyes, dripping fangs, and bloody claws of the dreaded bugbear.

And then there are the boogeymen; those nameless, faceless, shapeless menaces that lurk in dark closets and under beds. When you turn out the basement light, they silently glide out of every shadowy corner, treading on your heels as you run up the darkened staircase. We haven't the slightest idea what they are, where they came from, what they look like, or what they might do to us – but we fear them in the very marrow of our bones. They are the avatars of the Unknown, and their presence causes the hairs on the back of our necks to rise as we break out in a cold sweat. They are the reason we never look behind us going down dark hallways, the reason we avoid glancing in mirrors in dark rooms, and the reason we never let hand nor foot dangle off the edge of the bed.

Our lives are plagued by fear; fears of our own personal imaginings, fears impressed upon us by others, and even fears that we can't identify or adequately express to ourselves. These fears are weapons of the Devil, and he uses them quite effectively to prevent us from becoming the warriors God calls us to be. God consistently tells His people, "FEAR NOT!" The Devil whispers, "Watch out! Be careful!" God says, "Be strong and courageous!" The Devil says, "Do you have any idea what's out there...?" God says, "I am with you always." Satan sneers and hisses, "You are all alone now..."

Our hobgoblins cling to us like a foul odor. We fear we are not strong enough for what God asks us to do. We're afraid we don't understand His will for us, so we don't move forward. We're afraid others will misunderstand us, so we remain silent. We invent any number of fears that really have no basis until they manifest themselves in our own psyche, and the Devil latches onto these and laughs all the way to...nowhere. Because when we become paralyzed by hobgoblin fears, that's exactly where we're going. God wants us to move forward, to boldly proceed in His Word and rely on His grace for strength and His mercy for forgiveness; He doesn't like to see us restrained in the dark forest by a pack of screaming hobgoblins.

As the shadows lengthen, the bugbears emerge and block our path, and new fears arise. We're afraid of offending someone, so we don't speak out against wickedness. We're afraid of seeming like a hypocrite, so we pretend not to mind when our morals are violated. We're afraid of losing face with the world, so we hide our piety and adopt a secular attitude. God gives us an amazing light to shine before all the world, and the

> *"The wise man in the storm prays to God, not for safety from danger, but deliverance from fear."*
>
> *~Ralph Waldo Emerson*

first thing we do is look for a bushel-basket because we're drawing too much attention to ourselves. God would have us deny ourselves this cowardly retreat and let His Gospel light penetrate the darkest regions of our world.

Then, night falls, and our hair stands on end as the formless boogeymen glide silently out of their hiding places and creep up on us. *What is out there?* We're not sure. *What are we afraid of?* We don't know. The boogeymen whisk past our heads, causing us to whip around one direction and the other as we quicken our pace and miss opportunities for service with each hurried step. The Future. Career Changes. Family. Finances. Children. Old Age. Death. Anything that is unseen, unknown, we imagine as hideously terrifying and avoid it or hurry past. God asks us to trust Him, but our sinful nature would rather listen to the lies of the Devil; like a quivering child who is both repulsed and hopelessly fascinated by a horrific movie or ghost story.

Hobgoblins. Bugbears. Boogeymen. It seems that we're in for a very long night.

What is a child so beset by fearful monstrosities to do? What any child does when frightened beyond what his courage can endure; we cry out to our Father. He rushes into the room and flicks on the Light. Instantly, hope returns, and all of our irrational fears flee back into dark closets and under beds. How could we forget the strength of our Father? How could we be so silly to imagine that anything could ever hurt us with Him around? He sits down by us and puts His gentle hand on our head. His Light shines from friends and pastors who share the promises of Scripture with us. In the Light of His Word, it's hard to believe that we could ever be scared of the superficial terrors that plagued us moments ago.

Go ahead; sleep with the Light on. And remember that Father is always close by if we need to call for Him again. "He will cover you with his feathers, and under his wings you will find refuge; his faithfulness will be your shield and rampart. You will not fear the terror of night" (Psalm 91:4-5).

Chapter VIII
If Looks Could Kill: Medusas, Basilisks, and Other Eye-Catching Creatures

Dragons are certainly powerful and awe-inspiring creatures. Ghosts and ghouls are creepy and terrifying in their own right. But nothing carries the particular flavor of dread that we get from reading about creatures that can paralyze or kill with nothing more than a well-aimed glance.

Our eyes certainly have the capacity for getting us into trouble. Perhaps that is why humans have long recognized them as a weakness, especially when pitted against certain forces or temptations. While true beauty serves as an indicator of things wholesome and good in fantasy literature, superficial, illusory, or deceptive beauty often serves as the bait by which unwary adventurers are lured to their doom. Just as it is critically important for heroes to be able to distinguish between these two types of "beauty," it is equally important for us to be able to recognize and identify sins and temptations that enter into our brains through our eyeballs – and soon take control of our lives.

Of course, not everything that is harmful to us is beautiful, even on the surface. Some things are so offensive, so rank, so hideous and terrible to behold that viewing them causes irreparable harm to our spirit. These potent temptations don't even assume a pretense of external beauty, and they certainly aren't any prettier underneath. So how is it that anyone is taken in by their temptation and harmed, if they are so easy to recognize? Knowing the answers to these questions will help struggling heroes successfully navigate the lairs of these vile visual assassins and emerge with little worse than singed eyebrows. So put on your sunglasses and grab your mirror; they're waiting just around the next corner.

Worst. Hair Day. Ever.

Of all the monsters in mythology that hit you smack in the eye, none is of greater antiquity than Medusa the Gorgon sister. This little lady achieved household name status nearly overnight, with her big, beautiful, bulging eyes, soft green skin, and hair color so natural that only a herpetologist can tell for sure. Some versions of the myth record her as being born a hideous Gorgon, and other versions claim that Athena gave her an extreme make-over after discovering her romantic rendezvous with Poseidon. Either way, the end result was that Medusa was sporting razor claws, slimy scales, and a head full of hissing serpents instead of hair.

Of course, the most striking feature of Medusa was the profound impact she had on her many admirers. They became utterly speechless upon viewing her – in fact, they never spoke again. Anyone viewing Medusa's face was instantly turned to stone. So this Perseus fellow comes along and whacks off her head by sneaking up on her while she slept and looking in the reflection of his shield. That's when he discovers the really creepy thing; the head still petrifies people even after Medusa is dead. Oh, that and the fact that Pegasus and Chrysaor the warrior come bursting out of her body fully grown because she was pregnant by Poseidon and they couldn't naturally be born from her monster form ("Congratulations! Twins! A boy and a...flying horse...") – although this *does* add an interesting "death and rebirth" element to the story. Anyway, Perseus flies away with her head (he had some nifty winged sandals) and drips blood all over the place, creating nasty poisonous vipers and such in the process. Finally, Athena rids the world of the deadly head once and for all.

Initially, Medusa was a single entity; a lone, monstrous villain that starred in one of many Greek myths. Somehow, in modern fantasy literature and video games, a whole race of medusas has been spawned, and the term refers to a generic monster with the same attributes as the star of the original myth. Whenever one of these fearsome creatures in encountered, readers and gamers alike know one thing; don't look at her face!

So exactly what dangers does this figure of feminine fury represent to Christian readers? Are there certain sins or temptations that are so powerful

> *"But my eyes are fixed on you, O Sovereign Lord; in you I take refuge – do not give me over to death."*
>
> *~Psalm 141:8*

that merely glimpsing them will petrify the will and paralyze our ability to flee or react? Certainly drug use or other highly addictive behavior comes to mind (Will the peanut gallery please reserve their comments on "getting stoned"?). It doesn't take much to get hooked physically and psychologically, so trying it even "just once" could lock a person into a cycle of addiction that spirals into worse temptations. Once the chemical takes hold and the peer pressure kicks in, the will is petrified and rendered helpless to the addiction.

The face of Medusa must also represent those things which are so utterly detestable that we dare not even glance at them. Classically, Medusa's visage has been a symbol for the Devil himself, and dabbling with Satanism or the occult could certainly classify as extremely risky behavior. People start out with just a vague notion of curiosity, of "just wanting to look," and pretty soon they find that they are in further than they ever expected to be. The cautionary moral of the Medusa, then, is: "Don't look! Don't even glance! It'll be the last thing you ever do!" This same warning could be applied to many other sins and temptations as well.

For twentieth century Nihilists, Medusa's face had a different meaning. As die-hard atheists who believed that life has no meaning whatsoever, they refused to look too closely at many of the aspects of life. To do so would only

> *"Skepticism is a religion very rich in evangelists but very short on saviors."*
>
> ~Robert Brault

paralyze one with despair and misery, since there can be no hope, no assurance, and ultimately no free will since they believed that all human decisions were merely the product of our own environment and heredity. Once they were petrified by this devastating "reality," they would be rendered incapable of blissfully enjoying what pleasures life had to offer. While it is important for Christians to understand the beliefs and philosophies of our time so that we can witness to those around us, this same Medusa's warning might apply to us as well. Basically, it is this: Don't gaze too long into the empty human philosophies of our time. They are ever-changing deceptions of the Devil that lead only to shallow materialism or crushing despair. The Christian's life, however, is filled with introspection; gazing within ourselves to recognize our failures and shortcomings, sincerely repenting of them, and living a new and better life in the light of God's forgiveness.

I Spy With My Little Eye Something...Deadly

> Q: What do you get when you take a chicken's egg and hatch it under a toad?

> A: I don't know, but you'll probably croak when you look at it!

Actually, this is pretty close to the medieval recipe for two deadly (and fortunately, mythical) creatures. The basilisk was an extremely venomous serpent that could kill with a mere glance, and it was produced by taking a snake or toad egg and hatching it under a cockerel, or rooster. The cockatrice was very similar, except that it had wings and was produced by hatching an egg-bound cockerel beneath a snake or a toad. The existence of these two strange creatures was a well-documented fact in medieval Europe, and they even made appearances in scientific bestiaries of their day. It was said that the odor of a weasel and the sound of a rooster crowing were their fatal weaknesses, as well as seeing their own reflection in a mirror (which explains why their hair was always so messy).

The basilisk was reported to be so incredibly venomous that it literally oozed a trail of toxic vapor, killing the vegetation that it passed by and even splitting solid rocks. If it so much as breathed on any living thing, it meant instant death. In fact, Pliny the Elder said that its venom was so powerful that if a man on horseback killed the basilisk with a wooden spear, the poison would travel up the spear and kill the man who wielded it...*and* his horse! Oh yeah, and did I mention that if it looked at you, you'd die instantly? For obvious reasons, taxidermy was a particularly hazardous occupation in those days.

Later reports further enhance the deadly capacities of this raging, ruthless reptile. It was eventually said to be able to breathe fire, and even developed the ability to emit a fatal sound. Evidently, it had become somewhat of a laughing stock among travelers for its feeble ineffectiveness at hunting, and was forced to adapt a new modus operandi ("Ha! A basilisk, how pathetic! All we have to do is look away and it can't even hurt us. Hey, do you hear that sound? Gaacckkk!!!").

Basilisk, cockatrice, whatever; the point is, this thing was a killing machine. It was a slithering menace that dealt out death indiscriminately. Merchants and travelers actually carried concealed weasels and fully automatic roosters with them wherever they went as protection against the Grim Creeper. Centuries later, this reptilian Rambo retains his reputation in the pages of fantasy fiction and gaming lore.

Is there such an enemy in the world of the Christian warrior? Is there something or someone out there that oozes death wherever he goes, that breathes out toxic deception, and knows that the way to mankind's heart is straight through the eye? You know it – and he hasn't even changed his disguise. "Now the serpent was more crafty than any of the wild animals the Lord God had made. He said to the woman, 'Did God really say, 'You must not eat from any tree in the garden'?'" (Gen. 3:1). That's right; the old slithering snake is still out there to this day, breathing his deadly lies all around and leaving a trail of death and destruction in his wake.

> *"Telling us to obey instinct is like telling us to obey 'people.' People say different things: so do instincts. Our instincts are at war...Each instinct, if you listen to it, will claim to be gratified at the expense of the rest."*
>
> ~C.S. Lewis

His gaze falls upon us, and he knows just what to put in front of our eyes: "When the woman saw that the fruit of the tree was good for food and pleasing to the eye…she took some and ate it" (Gen. 3:6).

When Satan finds a tactic that works, he sticks with it. He knows that we have a weakness for things that look like they would satisfy the desires of our flesh. And because his "gaze attack" worked on our ancestors, we are already dead from the very beginning in our state of original sin. Although we have the antidote to his venomous breath and fatal stare through Christ's victory, he still tries every day to lure us with new gaze attacks in an attempt to weaken and destroy our faith or undermine our witness. We ought to take these assaults very seriously, because they have the potential to harm us terribly.

Jesus Himself warns, "I tell you that anyone who looks at a woman lustfully has already committed adultery with her in his heart. If your right eye causes you to sin, gouge it out and throw it away. It is better for you to lose one part of your body than for your whole body to be thrown into hell" (Matt. 5:28-29).

While I don't think Jesus is promoting self-mutilation here, I

> *"The will is a beast of burden. If God mounts it, it wishes and goes as God wills; if Satan mounts it, it wishes and goes as Satan wills; Nor can it choose its rider…the riders contend for its possession."*
>
> *~Martin Luther*

do think He is emphasizing the seriousness of sin and underscoring its terrible consequences. "But each one is tempted when, by his own evil desire, he is dragged away and enticed. Then after desire has conceived, it gives birth to sin; and sin, when it is full-grown, gives birth to death" (James 1:14-15). The natural consequences of even one sin would be eternal separation from God in hell. Thanks to Jesus' death and resurrection, our sins are removed from us by God's grace. Yet each time we allow our sinful desires to rule over us and drag us into sin, we risk the weakening of the faith by which we receive God's grace. Eventually, when sin gets a stranglehold on our life, we risk our faith being shattered by either a stubborn, unrepentant attitude that "I'm not really doing anything wrong, so I don't need God's forgiveness" or by a despairing conviction that "there's no way God could possibly forgive me, so I'll just run away from Him."

Satan knows that he can lure us into desire by means of our eyes, and this desire can lead to sin, and this sin can lead to death – even for Christians. That's why Jesus tells us to flee and avoid temptation at all costs. You'd run from a basilisk or cockatrice, so why flirt with something even more deadly – something that can destroy your very soul?

Simply Enchanting: Nymphs, naiads, and mind-altering beauty

"Do not lust in your heart after her beauty or let her captivate you with her eyes..."~Proverbs 6:25

Since we are on the subject of visual temptation...

It may surprise some readers to learn that feminine beauty has long been considered a carnal weakness for many men. Of course, we can't let the ladies completely off the hook either since they can be tempted by lust and physical attraction just as much as men. And we dare not mention that some unscrupulous females throughout history have even used their God-given physical beauty for less than savory purposes.

Yes, the physical and chemical attraction between man and woman is part of God's design for His creation. But like everything else that is touched by sin's curse, it can be used by the enemy to harm and deceive us as well. Literature is replete with instances of men or women acting irrationally out of character due to the influence of their sexual desires. This truism of reality is reflected in fantasy literature by several types of creatures that pose a significant threat to heroes and adventurers by means of their physical beauty and attractiveness.

Nymphs, naiads, dryads, sirens, and other sensual beauties populate the forests, rivers, and meadows of myth and fantasy, waiting to entice and befuddle any adventurer who happens along. While there are a few male counterparts to these mystical seductresses (see especially "vampires" in the next chapter), readers will note that most often these tempters take on female forms. I believe there are several reasons for that, and both sexes are welcome to take offense at any or all of the following explanations.

For one, literature has been more or less dominated by men throughout history, and male protagonists have *greatly* outnumbered heroines; ergo, creatures that pose a sexual temptation for the hero have tended to be female. Secondly – whether this is fair or not – men have generally been considered more prone to being dominated by their physical desires, and women have enjoyed a certain notoriety for their ability to entice and manipulate men through their sexuality. Additionally, the idea of men's philandering has always been at least slightly more socially acceptable than female promiscuity, and to present a male in the role of a nymph would have been considered downright obscene in many cultures. Lastly, women have simply been considered to possess more alluring or sensual qualities than men, the female form has generally been regarded as more graceful and elegant, and the (largely male) reading population throughout the centuries has probably simply preferred not to visualize groups of nude or scantily clad men frolicking in the forests and meadows or splashing about in springs and rivers.

The fact is females generally fit the bill when an author includes physical seduction as a theme. If the protagonist is female, I suppose a lusty young demigod or handsome satyr

269

would work nicely. However, since female protagonists themselves are quite rare, the "male seducer" archetype just hasn't become very common yet.

All readers can learn something valuable from the nymph archetype, however; regardless of gender. Whether male or female, God has created us to be naturally attracted to the opposite sex, and we all struggle from time to time with keeping that attraction within the confines of what is pleasing to Him. It is a sterling example of God's good creation being warped and corrupted by sin: God created sexual attraction to please His most precious creations, man and woman; Satan perverts and manipulates God's creation and His will for us; mankind abuses God's creation and uses it in a way that displeases Him out of sinful rebellion; mankind suffers temporal and eternal consequences for his act of rebellion. While the eternal consequences are the same for all sins, the temporal

> *"Her feet go down to death; her steps lead straight to the grave."*
>
> *~Proverbs 5:5*

consequences for sexual sin are myriad: broken relationships; anger and depression; jealousy; families torn apart; diseases; unplanned pregnancies; destroyed reputations; even suicide and murder. None of these things are God's will for us. His will is for a husband and wife to enjoy the physical and chemical attraction that He has built into us, only with each other and within the confines of marriage. How sad that our society rejects the truth that *this* is what leads to happiness and stability, not the perverse "freedoms" and sexual depredations that people today practice for the sake of finding "fulfillment."

Of course, there is a difference between *knowing* the path, and *walking* it. Many Christians (and even non-Christians) realize the possible consequences of succumbing to sexual temptation, but still put themselves willingly into situations that soon lead to the abandonment of all self-control. Sexual temptation is a powerful force. Too powerful, perhaps? Is it so strong that some people are simply "unable" to control their lust? Not at all. The truth is, God always provides a way out of temptation, but our bodies *want* to go ahead and tumble down the slippery slope of sinful behavior. Sure, we love God and want to please Him; we just enjoy pleasing ourselves *more*. And somehow, our brains stop working when passion and desire well up inside us; we tend to forget about "consequences" and what will happen tomorrow. That's the sort of thing *God* would probably think about.

> *"Lust is to the other passions what the nervous fluid is to life; it supports them all, lends strength to them all: ambition, cruelty, avarice, revenge, are all founded on lust."*
>
> *~Marquis De Sade*

Many a reputation, career, family, and ministry have been ruined by the influence of sexual temptation. Countless heroes have been irreversibly detoured from their God-given journeys so that they could frolic with the naiads or dance with the apple nymphs. Tragically, these heroes are never seen again; their quests go unfulfilled and the world loses another valuable warrior as the forces of evil are allowed to surge to new levels. The seductresses of myth and fantasy teach a valuable lesson about self-control and fleeing temptation.

Human beings are particularly prone to sexual temptation since it involves the physical, psychological, and spiritual aspects of humanity. This is added to the extremely addictive nature of sexual sins combined with an unparalleled attitude of permissiveness in our society to create a veritable recipe for disaster. To make matters worse, Chef Boy-are-we-evil Satan keeps tossing sinners into his steaming cauldron of consequences and stewing up a nice batch of despair and hopelessness. Every day, new victims swallow this toxic broth which dissolves life and faith from the inside out. The Church must remain ever vigilant, proclaiming God's good and gracious will for us through the Law and swiftly administering the antidote to Satan's poison stew – the Gospel of Christ's cross.

Chapter IX
Chronic Coffin: Perils of the undead

Mankind has been terrorized for centuries by the idea of the dead returning in horrible, mutilated form with the sole purpose of plaguing the living. Nearly every culture throughout the world has myths and legends revolving around deceased humans coming back to haunt their enemies, families, or communities in either physical or metaphysical form. Even today, the majority of the population in many parts of the world holds fast to the belief in ghosts or other undead creatures that just can't seem to "rest in peace." The preoccupation with the not-quite-departed even leads some adults to take protective measures against unwanted undead intrusion, not to mention serving as the source of unnumbered nocturnal fears for children everywhere.

If hobgoblins, bugbears, and boogeymen draw their power from the fear of the unknown, then the undead are a manifestation of the deepest, most widely-held anxiety over something beyond human understanding. For unbelievers, this is a natural result of the darkness that looms beyond their ephemeral mortal lifespan. No matter how satisfying or fulfilling they believe their life to be, they cannot hide from the fact that death could be looming around every corner, and the prospect of an eternity of oblivion is something that the human mind has difficulty coming to terms with. Sadly, peaceful oblivion would be much better than the eternal torments which await those who die apart from the hope of Jesus' forgiveness and mercy.

Unfortunately, many Christians share this uncertainty about death and become just as anxious as the pagan world over the prospect of their own mortality. This fear betrays a lack of trust in God's promise that we are saved by faith alone, and need not fret over our own merits or worthiness. It also shows how little faith we have in God's assurance to care for those whom we are leaving behind on this earth. For Christians, death ought to be nothing more than the gateway to eternal paradise and freedom from all our earthly cares and worries, not simply another apprehension to plague us during this life. It should be a time for rejoicing in the power of Christ's resurrection and the entrance of our loved ones into everlasting bliss, even while we mourn for the loss of their continued love and companionship.

The fears and concerns we have surrounding death are portrayed in myth and fantasy by undead creatures of all varieties. These macabre monsters serve as avatars of the grave – the ultimate consequence of mankind's rebellion to God and our fiercest primal foe. Death is not a natural part of God's creation, and the distorted and harrowing nature of undead creatures in film and literature reflects the enmity with which we regard death at the core of our being. While each type of undead creature may represent some unique aspect of humanity or reveal a specific truth about the human condition, all of them stem from the fatal curse of sin and reveal the horrible consequences of our separation from God.

1. Grave Danger: Zombies, Ghouls, and Skeletons

The corporeal undead hold a special place in the pages of fantasy fiction, and the last few decades have seen a rise in interest in these *revenants* (from a Latin word meaning "to return") that borders on obsession. Undead creatures that retain their physical corpses represent the very real, tangible aspects of death. It is through them that death stalks the streets and alleys of the human psyche, reminding mankind of his own mortality and the dread that accompanies death, this strange foreigner. These undead creatures present death as a personal foe, but also as a global menace – one that no one can escape.

The Skeleton: Death's poster child

Skeletons have been used as a universal symbol of death in many cultures for untold centuries. Skulls adorn chemical receptacles, restricted areas, and so forth, warning us of deadly poisons or other lethal hazards. The empty eye sockets, sunken cheekbones, and ghastly grimace combine to create a chilling portrait of decay and finality. Even the personification of death itself – the Grim Reaper – most often appears in skeletal form. When the last vestiges of life have been stripped away from humanity, all that remains is a bare skeleton – a grisly reminder of what we are to eventually become and what lies beneath the soft, warm flesh of every human being.

Skeletons in fantasy fiction and games are harbingers of death. They are feared not because of their lethal fighting skills or supernatural abilities; they really don't have any other than holding themselves together and walking upright without the advantage of a system of muscles and ligaments. No, the real terror that they incite comes from their unnatural state itself and the foreshadowed doom of the hero becoming just another skeletal warrior in the armies of darkness. They are the remains of previous adventurers who failed in their tasks and now hunt the living.

Skeletons never grow weary, never need to sleep or eat, do not think, and are relentless in their pursuit of their living targets. Some skeletons encountered in fantasy fiction are mindlessly autonomous, seeking out any living creature and killing it simply because that is their nature – and perhaps as a means of self-replication. Other skeletons are animated to their unnatural state of undeath by means of baleful magic, becoming the plodding slaves of a wicked necromancer (see Chapter III). These kinds of skeletons are

> *"The cords of death entangled me, the anguish of the grave came upon me; I was overcome by trouble and sorrow."*
>
> *~Psalm 116:3*

particularly dangerous, as they are organized with a single, sinister purpose by an intelligent master. Skeletons are not usually quick or agile, but they attack in overwhelming numbers. When solitary, their terrifying appearance – and their tendency to emerge theatrically in horrifying fashion from locations such as swamps and graves – often paralyzes their victims with fright.

It is not uncommon for Christians to fall victim to their "skeletons" – aspects of their past that come back to haunt them. Perhaps someone struggles with accepting forgiveness for a sin from long ago because of the ongoing temporal consequences. Or maybe the temptation that leads to that sin is a recurring struggle in their life. Sometimes, although a Christian has long ago been forgiven of a sin and moved on, that error continues to haunt their life and hinder their ministry. Though we may fight these skeletons all our life, they will continue to respawn and replicate, making our personal battles and overall mission very difficult.

In addition to these personal skeletons, Christian warriors face many foes along their journey that bear the face of death. We are often stricken with doubt and fear when we recognize our own weaknesses in an adversary, and even more frightening is the thought of what we may become should we fail our mission and be overcome by Satan. We see the mocking grins on the death mask of those who have fallen from the faith and instinctively seek to drag other warriors down with them. Their fate is both tragic and horrifying; their own spiritual death causes all the fear and doubt that we have been fighting against to come bubbling to the surface. It causes us to question our own strength and abilities as Christians, thinking, "If someone like *him* could lose faith, what will happen to me?"

That's exactly the danger of encountering the skeletal remains of deceased warriors; we put our faith in our own strength and rely on that to overcome the obstacle they present to us. *They* may have been very strong during their life as Christians, and that fills us with a sense of doom and foreboding. In order to overcome such trials, we must abandon our own feeble efforts and turn the battle over to the God of Light in whom we trust. We must pray to Him for guidance and receive *His* strength. The Light of His Gospel will burst through the gloom, and the derisive grins of our skeletal attackers will be turned away as they flee to their shallow graves and murky swamps. God's Light is so powerful that, sometimes, one of these foes will be allowed to shake off the cold, clammy shackles of undeath, be regenerated with renewed flesh and spirit, and once again join the battle with greater strength than they ever knew previously. We must continue to bring His Light to all such creatures; not just as our own defense, not just as a weapon of extermination, but as the cure and reversal of their terrible state.

> *"Dry bones, hear the word of the Lord…I will make breath enter you, and you will come to life."*
>
> ~Ezekiel 37:4-5

The Zombie: A spreading contagion of apocalyptic proportions

There is something particularly profane about the walking corpse that thrills and terrifies the masses. While the skeleton serves as the mask of death, the zombie retains the vestiges of life in the tattered bits of flesh that still cling to its face and body. It is fully distinguishable as death, but as the same time eerily lifelike and recognizable as a former vessel of life. Especially terrifying is the aspect of a former friend or companion, now hideous and terrible in animated death.

Like the skeleton, the zombie is an undead creature that operates out of either mindless malevolence or mindless obedience to a necromancer overlord. They are typically no more dexterous than skeletons, but move with the same plodding inevitability that renders their victims frantic or helpless. The skeleton has a certain cleanliness to its whitewashed bones and skull, picked clean and devoid of all traces of former life and appearance. The zombie, however, is covered in tattered bits of decaying flesh and accompanied by the foul odor of decomposition. It is "unclean" in every sense of the word, and all the more terrifying because of its "fresh" state – all too recently, it could breathe, talk, and laugh with other human beings. But most horrifying of all, the zombie pursues its quarry not only out of an innate sense of malice, but also to feed on the flesh and blood of its living prey. And when it has eaten its fill, the victim will also rise and join the ranks of the zombie plague.

Zombies are not just a solitary, individual threat. Through their insatiable hunger and rapid self-replication, they pose a threat to the entire global community. As the strength and numbers of humanity dwindle and diminish, the power of the zombie horde grows and multiplies. They are silent, restless, and unrelenting; their advent could easily spell the doom of all mankind – an idea that has been portrayed in the plethora of "zombie apocalypse" books and movies recently.

The world is filled with spiritually dead zombies; walking corpses who mindlessly follow whatever hunger strikes them at the moment. They can never be satisfied because their state of spiritual death results in an emptiness that they mistakenly try to mollify with worldly goods or pleasure. The truth is, their insatiable appetite grows larger the more they feed, like the she-wolf from Dante's *Inferno*. The "flesh of the living" represents not only all the carnal lusts and material possessions in this life, but also the true peace and joy experienced by the living – Christian men and women.

> *"What a wretched man I am! Who will deliver me from this body of death? Thanks be to God – through Jesus Christ our Lord!"*
>
> *~Romans 7:24-25*

The idea of enmity between the living and undead is nothing new, nor is it more fitting in any other case than that of the zombies that populate this world. Those who are dead in their unbelief will naturally seek to feed on the life of faithful Christians; but even this will not provide true life or sustenance for them. And they are certainly capable of spreading their cursed disease of undeath as they bite and infect other Christians with their lies, misleading philosophies, and lifeless existence. In this age of rampant secular humanism, it's easy for Christians to believe that we are in the midst of a true "zombie apocalypse." Their numbers and strength seem to be growing stronger daily as more of our kind fall victim to the curse of faithless undeath.

> *"For if, by the trespass of the one man, death reigned through that one man, how much more will those who receive God's abundant provision of grace and the gift of righteousness reign in life through the one man, Jesus Christ."*
>
> *~Romans 5:17*

Christian warriors must always be on their guard against the dangers of these deadly foes. Though sluggish and clumsy, they are unrelenting in their wearisome pursuit, and are capable of sneaking up on us in dark corridors or feeding on us as we sleep. We must never drop our vigilance, because before we know it they will gather in sufficient numbers to storm the very fortress of the Church and tear down its walls. This is

281

exactly what they seek to do, though they could never know or admit it. They are mindlessly controlled by Satan, their dark overlord, and his ultimate plan is the utter destruction of the living race.

The Sword of the Spirit shines brightly in the darkness. No zombie can bear that light, and no warrior can be taken unawares where that blade flashes its radiant warning. Hold it out before you at all times. Use it to strike down the assault of those who would ravenously devour your life. At the least, you will clear your own path and be able to continue along your journey. At best, you will free these pitiful creatures from their dreary undead prison, giving them an opportunity to taste the peace and joy of *real* life; life that is found only in Christ.

Too Cool for Ghoul: Protecting the dead from their own

As bad as an undead creature feeding on the flesh of the living sounds, the feeding habits of the ghoul are even more repulsive. Ghouls are usually regarded as undead, although some cultures and myths identified them as actual living creatures, which would make their diet of corpse flesh all the more disturbing in nature. Either way, knowing the background behind these vermin makes a person realize how serious it is to accuse someone of "ghoulish" behavior.

There are certainly those among the spiritually dead who would harm and devour their own kind. Of course, they wouldn't scruple to viciously attack a living soul if it ventured into their territory – especially if they interrupt meal time. So the answer for Christians is simply to stay away from areas where the dead congregate, right? Unfortunately, our mission isn't that simple. As Jesus said, "It is not the healthy who need a doctor, but the sick" (Mark 2:17) and "No one lights a lamp and hides it in a jar or puts it under a bed. Instead, he puts it on a stand, so that those who come in can see the light" (Luke 8:16).

> *"Love your enemies and pray for those who persecute you."*
>
> *~Matthew 5:44*

It is a frightening prospect, but God has called us not only to our own survival, but to bring light and life to those who are dead in sin. Our path leads into the cemeteries, graveyards, and mausoleums of this world, and there we find that the dead are not even safe from themselves. As we hold out the antidote for their unnatural death, we are also called to protect and defend the dead from their own ghoulish counterparts, even if they refuse the life-given draught we offer them. In fact, honor would demand just such a course of action, even if we found their tormentors to be among the living – our very own.

The Lich: Death's Deadliest

The third chapter of this book discussed various magic users and their archetypes, distinguishing their motives and means of magical prowess. The section on the "necromancer" archetype alluded to a type of magic user who would willingly choose a state of undeath in order to prolong their existence and obtain unparalleled levels of arcane knowledge and power. These undead sorcerers are called "liches," and they are one of the most dangerous undead figures in all of fantasy.

> *"Before we acquire great power we must acquire wisdom to use it well."*
>
> *~Ralph Waldo Emerson*

Though a lich is usually corporeal in nature, he is significantly more difficult to destroy than your average skeleton or zombie. He is protected by magical spells and barriers that are not penetrated by swords or arrows. He commands legions of lesser undead who surround and protect him. But most of all, he retains his intelligence, his wicked character, and his own malicious will. He is cunning and crafty, possessing the "wisdom" of many more years than most mortal men could ever obtain. Despite the fact that his wisdom is cracked and flawed (like the evil sorcerer archetype), he poses a dire threat to the hero and his world.

Some liches even go on to abandon the physical body nearly completely, reducing their corporeal state to little more than a floating skull. This phenomenon betrays the fact that their true power does not lie in weapons or strength as men know it, but in their own foul craft and the secrets their evil sorcery that they employ in the cause of general destruction and mayhem. It also foreshadows the difficulty with which they must be slain. For even if a hero finds a way to destroy a lich's final physical form, their spirit remains unharmed – bound to this world by means of a "phylactery," a small physical object that receives their spirit or life-force after the body is abandoned. Unless the phylactery is identified and destroyed prior to the lich's defeat, they will simply regenerate or possess a new body each time they are routed.

There are some spiritually dead enemies in our world who are frightening in their strength and wicked lore. These are men and women who at one time served God, but have turned their backs on Him forever. They have been gifted with extreme intelligence, charisma, leadership, or some other extraordinary ability; but the Devil has enticed them away from the service of their Savior and drawn them into unnatural bondage and undeath. They gather to themselves armies of followers who mindlessly follow their subtle lies. Their true power lies in the influence they have with the world and with (especially) young Christian men and women. They inhabit schools, universities, courtrooms, political offices, stages, movie sets, and sometimes even church buildings.

Christian warriors must be extremely careful when planning an assault on such a foe. For even if the enemy can be defeated and their immediate influence overcome, their "spirit" will live on in their teachings and corrupt doctrines. First, the battle must focus on rooting out and shattering the foundation of their lies; whatever heresy they are proclaiming must be brought to light and smashed to bits with the hammer of God's Word. Only then will their teachings forever be defeated and their minions freed from their control. Proclaiming Scripture in truth and purity is the only means we have to fight these dreadnaughts of the undead.

2. Ghosts, Wraiths and Spectres: Unearthing the Substance Behind the Spooks (Ethereal or Imaginary)

While corporeal undead creatures present a concrete, tangible horror, the physical damage they can do often pales in comparison to the psychological horror presented by an ethereal foe. Though skeletons and zombies are certainly visually disturbing, a person can at least hope to defend himself by hacking the aberration to pieces. But malevolent apparitions constitute an intangible and seemingly indomitable threat; a fact which reflects the cold inevitability of death.

> *"I don't know that there are haunted houses. I know that there are dark staircases and haunted people."*
>
> *~Robert Brault*

Spectral enemies simply can't be defeated by traditional weapons. Heroes and adventurers sometimes find it necessary to venture far out of their way to find a way to overcome their ethereal nemeses. Quite often, this involves a whole separate quest where the hero faces further dangers and obstacles, but also gains new skills, abilities, or wisdom (in the spirit of the "seemingly aimless roaming" pattern). Other times, a force beyond the hero's abilities is required to defeat the ghostly enemy, requiring the hero to seek out a wizard or obtain a magical weapon. Sometimes the hero must perform an elaborate task or meet certain conditions – such as returning stolen treasure to its rightful owner or finding and exhuming remains for proper burial – in order to appease the spirit. There may even be times when the hero is simply forced to flee and find a way around the obstacle, something which can serve as a valuable dose of medicine for the hero's own hubris.

While not all ghosts in myth and fantasy are flagrantly malignant toward the hero, there is one type of ethereal foe that is ceaselessly malicious – the wraith. Wraiths are dark and vengeful creatures, and they wreak their vengeance upon everyone and everything that comes within reach rather than directing it toward a specified target. They are the remnants of particularly wicked individuals, and remain in death as they were in life. Wraiths remain bound to this world out of jealousy, greed, or pure spite.

The jealous wraith seeks and pursues enemies or sometimes even lovers from their lifetime, accosting anyone who happens to get in the way as they do so. Greedy wraiths generally remain in a certain location, guarding some treasure, valued possession, or significant locale from thieves and intruders in much the same way that dragons maintain a vigil over hoarded treasure that is quite useless to them. And then there are the wraiths who remain in this world simply because their spirits have become so cruel and wicked that even death will not deter them from continuing to inflict harm upon the world around them.

The lack of a corporeal body suggests that these ethereal enemies represent challenges and threats beyond what mere humans are capable of. To a Christian warrior, they are "the rulers...the authorities... the powers of this dark world and...the spiritual forces of evil in the heavenly realms" (Eph. 6:12). Like all other undead creatures, they are avatars of spiritual death whose very nature compels them to drain the life from any available victims.

Christians sometimes face challenges that simply can't be resolved through conventional means. Our powers of persuasion, logic, diplomacy, and even kindness will sometimes fall short in the effort to negotiate certain obstacles. Perhaps it's a sinful, resistant attitude in a friend or family member. Sometimes it doesn't even involve another person. Satan can attack us in ways we simply can't evade or defend against by our own strength; through sickness, disaster, or other unforeseeable tragedy.

At times like these, we need to know that it is unwise for us to tackle every situation using our own strength, wisdom, or abilities. It may take the help of others. It may require years of careful planning and painstakingly slow progress. Many times, it may simply require a "magic weapon" found only through prayer and God's direct intervention.

We must remember that these deadly and overwhelming ethereal threats are not invincible. They may require patience and resourcefulness. They may require much more effort and attention than we are initially willing to put forth since they are merely "side quests" that distract from the bigger picture. Sometimes they may even force us to swallow our pride and flee, at least for the time being. But we have help available through powerful friends and allies, and especially from our Lord and King, which enables us to eventually lay even these foes to rest and move on with our journey.

3. Bad Vampire/Good Vampire: Inverting a Classic Paradigm of Evil

It seems these days that a person can't swing a dead bat in the "Young Adult" section of the bookstore without being buried in paperbacks featuring handsome, romantic, misunderstood vampires. At the risk of sounding quite patronizing to my younger readers (I really am sorry about that), the affinity of teenagers with the "vampire" figure is quite understandable. There is something about the adolescent years that compels young people to identify with the "outsider" character archetype, especially if this character is estranged or even oppressed by society. Somehow, the vampire figure has gone from being a paradigm of evil to becoming a victim of unfortunate circumstances and closed-minded traditionalists.

Of course, the deadliest deception ever conceived by the Devil was to convince modern man that he is harmless; indeed, even nonexistent. So it should not surprise us to find a classical archetype for evil transmuting into more of a "tragic hero" than any kind of villain in these foolish times. Just as the devil has been caricatured down to a laughable (and even *lovable*?) little imp, we see the vicious, malevolent, parasitic, unnatural, immoral vampire getting in touch with his feelings and longing for understanding and human companionship. Pardon my language, but what a load of *crap*.

This mode of thinking is not only preposterous, it's downright dangerous. To teach our children that the Devil is no more than a laughingstock who is not to be taken seriously is like giving them a rattlesnake and saying, "Here, kids, play with this jump-rope" or "We replaced the sand on the playground with broken glass because it's shinier." The same mentality that marginalizes the malevolence of the vampire is gradually rendering all evil nonexistent in our world. Only the evil hasn't changed (if anything, it's grown); we've simply chosen to apply a different label or ignore it completely. You can imagine where this is going: "We're not going to call them 'terrorists' anymore. 'Oppositional political theorists' sounds much better."

The vampire of classical antiquity was opposed to every healthy and natural aspect of humanity. Since their first appearance about four centuries ago, the vampire has continued to grow in wickedness and take on new abhorrent powers and characteristics. By the mid twentieth century, at the height of their existence as a unified character archetype, vampires contained any or all of the following attributes:

- undead body which resists normal decomposition
- aversion or weakness to garlic, silver, and holy symbols
- ability to assume the form of certain animals (especially bats, rats, or wolves) or even assume the form of mist/shadow
- lack of reflection in mirrored surfaces
- inability to cross running water
- urge and necessity to feed on the blood of the living
- ability to charm victims or use illusion to appear handsome/attractive
- obsessive-compulsive disorder or arithmomania
- ability to create slave vampires out of their victims
- extreme aversion to daylight sometimes even resulting in total destruction
- susceptibility to decapitation, incineration, or impalement by wooden stakes
- immunity to natural aging; a form of limited immortality

In addition to these attributes, vampires differed from other forms of corporeal undead in that they retained their personality, intelligence, and free will (much like a lich), only their personality would become tainted and corrupted by the curse of vampirism and their free will was bound to whatever vampire "created" them. However, once a person became a vampire, they were quite literally "dead," and their soul departed to the afterlife leaving only a sentient undead body behind – unlike a lich, who willingly binds his soul to his undead body.

> *"For every bodiless spirit you encounter, there is a spiritless body you really don't want to run across."*
>
> *~Robert Brault*

The vampire archetype represents a particularly deadly type of sin in our world; a category of sin which is also becoming increasingly lethal as it gains more "acceptance" and "understanding" in our society. A vampire charms and seduces his victims, causing them to believe he is handsome or attractive when in fact he is a hideous undead aberration. In the same way, certain sins "charm" their victims, causing the poor host to fall hopelessly in love with his or her own fatal behavior. They eventually reach a point where they would aggressively defend their beloved captor, lashing out at anyone who suggests that the vampire sin is something that may be harmful to them. They cling desperately to this sin, until they are utterly enslaved by it; at which point the sin drains the last few ounces of life from them and casts them aside.

While everyone else around them can see how hideous, disgusting, and harmful the sinful behavior is, the victim persists in careening headlong into destruction. No amount of persuasion or intervention can stop the deadly indulgence, and attempts to do so usually result in bitterness and estrangement from the victim. Tragically, the life of the victim is lost (either physically, spiritually, or both) and the cycle of infection and transmission is spread and repeated in the process.

Vampires are not to become objects of pity. They are not capable of giving or receiving love. They are crafty, intelligent creatures capable of many forms of deception, shifting from corporeal to ethereal at will. They have few weaknesses and many immunities. Their destruction requires careful planning and delicate precision, or their would-be victims will be lost in the attempt. The best defense is general public education; all Christians need to know how to identify them and be willing to listen to friends and family who counsel them against falling prey to such creatures.

Chapter X
Demons and Devils: Exorcising Extreme Caution

One of the most prominent Christian authors of the last century, C.S. Lewis, writes in his *Screwtape Letters* a series of correspondence from Screwtape (an elder demon) to his nephew and fledgling tempter, Wormwood. When Wormwood enquires whether it would be better to make himself known to his victim (or "patient," as Screwtape calls him), Screwtape says that it would be better to "keep him in the dark," offering this advice:

> "The fact that 'devils' are predominantly comic figures in the modern imagination will help you. If any faint suspicion of your existence begins to arise in his mind, suggest to him a picture of something in red tights, and persuade him that since he cannot believe in that (it is an old textbook method of confusing them) he therefore cannot believe in you."

It doesn't take a very thorough browsing of any internet discussion board on the topic of religion to find how devastatingly effective this tactic has been in the last century. It seems that in our time, Satan has set aside his own vanity for the sake of winning souls. Our "enlightened" generation finds the notion of demons and devils luring and devouring human souls downright ridiculous, many Christians included. Belief in devils and demons as literal entities that seek our spiritual and physical destruction is steadily declining.

But perhaps even more disturbing is the newest perception on demons that has come into literature and film recently – the concept of the demon (or even Satan himself) as a kind of "tragic hero." Given the vast similarities and connections between demon and vampire folklore, it shouldn't be surprising that the two character models share this attribute. Recently, demons in fiction and pop culture have become much more powerful and menacing than the predominant caricature that is scorned and ridiculed. While in this regard they much more closely resemble actual demons, they veer violently off as their characters are developed as ambivalent to good and evil, often even forming benign relationship with humans. Rather than rebels against all that is good and pure in God's creation, they have become wandering castaways searching for meaning and happiness. God becomes the wicked One for pronouncing His just punishment on those who sought to overthrow Him (and us), and the demons and devils are to be pitied for their tragic condition of exile.

> *"There is no neutral ground in the universe; every square inch, every split second, is claimed by God and counter-claimed by Satan."*
>
> ~C.S. Lewis

Of course, the most frequent fear that parents have regarding their children's exposure to "demon literature" is that their kids will develop a fascination with demonology, Satanism, or other forms of the occult. While this is certainly a possible outcome – especially for those youngsters who lack a strong Christian background or do not have parents who guide them in their lives and reading choices – it doesn't present nearly the threat to their faith that the two modes of thinking just described can pose. As our society becomes more and more secularized, belief in *anything* supernatural tends to fall quickly out of vogue. While interest in demons and the Devil isn't something that should be marginalized as a tactic of the enemy, Satan is gathering far more converts to unbelief through people doubting that these infernal beings exist at all – and by direct correlation, disbelieving in the existence of an all-powerful and all-loving God.

But it gets even worse. Today's society isn't seeing *only* the apathy and indifference to God and His Word that has been increasing over the last century. There is also an open *hostility* toward God and the Church that is growing very rapidly. God is being perceived as the enemy in many people's lives. They would prefer to identify with the demons of modern fantasy fiction; they are the rebels who simply want to be rulers of their own destiny and resent a God who sets rules and guidelines for their lives. Never mind the fact that God only places these expectations on us for our own good, so that we can live a happy, healthy, peaceful, and fulfilling life; they see the only path to fulfillment as being one that pursues whatever carnal and spiritual instincts happen to blossom in front of them. Satan pulls a one-two punch; he hits them with temptation, drawing them away from God's will for us, then whispers lies in their ears so that they blame God for the consequences of their own rebellion.

Personally, I don't have a problem with demons and devils appearing in fantasy fiction and games – so long as they are true to reality. They should be evil, self-centered villains who care about nothing and no one except their own advancement. They are powerful and influential in our world, but ultimately defeated and impotent when faced with the Word of God. As long as their characters act in accordance with what we know to be accurate about them, demons in film and literature can only reinforce the true notion that there is a cosmic battle between good and evil occurring all around us. And that's something that deals a crushing blow to a much larger enemy today – spiritual skepticism and atheism.

From a "Christian warrior" standpoint, what could make a better arch-nemesis for a hero in story or game than a wicked, plotting demon? As young Christians grow and become accustomed with the real physical dangers and spiritual threats that they will be faced with in the world, their parents and teachers should not neglect to prepare them for the warfare that Satan will wage on them – simply because he knows the potential threat they present to his dastardly work. A story or game with a demonic villain serves as a great parallel to their own struggles against temptation, sin, and all the difficulties that come with living in a fallen world. It could be just the thing they need to inspire them, giving them drive to go out and kick Satan's tail. A little courage goes a long way in anyone's faith journey.

As for the unbelieving population, they can only benefit from one more influence in their lives showing them that the problems of this world have a specific spiritual root. The reality of the Devil and his cohorts has been swept aside for too long, and we are reaping the consequences in a world of ever-diminishing faith. A frightening number of individuals claiming to be Christians do not believe in Hell, demons, or the Devil (then what did Jesus die for, exactly?). Even more surprisingly, many members of the "Church of Satan" do not believe in an actual "Devil," but merely adopt him as their symbol of rebellion and self-gratification. I would posit that for many of them, belief in demons and devils would cause a drastic reconsideration of their faith values. But Satan is happy to sit back and fly under the radar these days, letting people gradually drift away from God and spirituality and toward materialism and sensuality. As the demon

> *"There are a thousand hacking at the branches of evil to one who is striking at the root."*
>
> ~Henry David Thoreau

Screwtape says in C.S. Lewis' *The Screwtape Letters*, "It is funny how mortals always picture us as putting things into their minds; in reality our best work is done by keeping things out."

Demons and devils can serve an important role in literature by serving as villains who are clearly evil. Too many antagonists today reflect the existentialist notion that absolute good and evil do not really exist. There is always a grey area where the hero finds himself suddenly in shadowy territory where right and wrong seem to overlap. While this can sometimes serve as a positive example of "seemingly aimless wandering" where the hero eventually comes to understand that there *is* a right and wrong course of action, too often it ends with a radical shift in the hero's value system where he becomes "enlightened" with post-modern nihilistic dogma.

Children absolutely *need* stories that clearly differentiate between right and wrong, good and evil, holy and profane. These values are universal spiritual absolutes, a fact which many adults today doubt (so I guess it isn't just children who need this kind of hero/villain relationship).

> *"If there were no good or evil, we would still need God in order to have true or false."*
>
> *"If there be no God, then what is truth but the average of all lies."*
>
> *~Robert Brault*

If demons or devils are included in games, movies, or literature, they should be distinctly evil characters and not some renegade tragic hero. Evil actions should result in consequences or punishment, and good should ultimately be vindicated. I know, we don't always see this occur in our lives; but then again we rarely see the final outcome of any interaction we have with other people. Most importantly, good should always triumph over evil in the end. Of course there will be pain and sacrifice along the way, but this final victory is a vital parallel to the most important truth in our world; Jesus Christ is the conqueror over sin, death, and the Devil. While we still struggle with difficulties in our lives, and while Satan manages to lure away many souls, we can rest assured that ultimately the cosmic war has been won and our victory is sealed through faith in Him.

Whatever shifting philosophies rage through the pages of books in the years to come, the reality of Christ's cross will outlive, outlast, and outshine all of the lies that are conceived by Satan and his minions. God's story for mankind's salvation will remain imprinted upon the hearts of all. And you can bet that this incredible theme will continue to burst forth gloriously in the stories of yesterday, today, and tomorrow.

Chapter XI
Navigating the Maze of Books, Movies and Games:
In the World, but not *of* it...

Each day when I read the newspaper, I realize something. Every time I turn on the television set, it becomes crystal clear. Sometimes this realization hits just by being out in public and seeing some of the people, advertisements, and social ideas that are out there. Every day affords an opportunity for me to see for myself that They are finally here.

Yes, the "dark times" have arrived.

It's scary to think about the potentially disastrous road that our world is on right now. It's true that we live in a very exciting era where science and medicine have provided unparalleled comforts and conveniences, where new advances, developments, and discoveries are being announced every day, and where travel and communication have connected the countries of the world into one dynamic organism. Yet it is these very comforts, advances, and connections that make the world such a scary place.

> *"I think everybody should get rich and famous and do everything they ever dreamed of so they can see that it's not the answer."*
>
> ~*Jim Carrey*

History shows us all too clearly how easily Satan twists and manipulates the good things of this world and uses them to his own advantage. Our modern conveniences have fed our apathy, slothfulness, and greed. The developments and discoveries of the past century have quickly been converted to use for selfish, sinful, destructive purposes. The modern network of travel and communication has indeed brought the world together – in a veritable tower of Babel project. Satan now has the resources at his disposal to disseminate his bile constantly and effectively. It's enough to make a Christian parent ready to pack up their kids and head for the mountains, adopting the ascetic lifestyle of a hermit. Is that the answer? Is that what God would want us to do at a time like this?

Tolkien's *Lord of the Rings* saga asks that very question. With orcs and goblins, wraiths and necromancers closing in, should the sylvan races flee to safety in some far off land? Do we abandon this world as lost and leave those who remain behind to struggle hopelessly on their own? Any die-hard fantasy fan would respond to this question with a resounding "No! We must stay and fight!" And that alone is enough to tell me that fantasy fiction can't be all bad.

As dark and depressing as these times may seem, we have to realize that the dark times have been with us since that fateful consumption of the fruit in Eden. Since then, God in His grace has always provided warriors, wizards, dwarves, and elves in sufficient number to stem the tides of evil that swell upon our flanks. He has always given us the strength and courage necessary to stand up for His truth and shine the light of His Word in the dark world, no matter how bleak things may look at times. When the struggles and temptations of this world and its present darkness threaten to overwhelm us, we can trust the promise that God is sustaining and even strengthening us, preparing us for even greater service to Him. "We also rejoice in our sufferings, because we know that suffering produces perseverance; perseverance, character; and character, hope" (Romans 5:3-4).

The foremost theme in all of fantasy fiction, the "Hero's Journey" motif, teaches Christians that everything happens to us for a reason. Satan converts good things into evil, and God takes that intended evil and bends it right back into good. All of the trials and obstacles that the Devil throws at us are really only training and strengthening God's children, enabling stout-hearted warriors to push back against his wicked advances. "No, in all these things we are more than conquerors through him who loved us" (Romans 8:37). Satan would use our sufferings and losses to tear us away from God, but our Savior uses these things to draw us even closer to Himself.

So we take our stand, feet firmly planted on the foundation of Christ's victory on our behalf. Whatever battles we face in this world, we do so with the knowledge and faith that our greatest foes are already cast down and vanquished. A crown of glory awaits at the end of the journey, bought with the blood of the Prince of Peace. He will guide us through the forest of life, bringing us at last to His Father's home, in whose kingdom will we rest forever.

Be a Wise and Helpful Guide

If you've picked up this book hoping to find a list of current fantasy titles accompanied by a "Good" or "Evil" box checked off next to each one, now is the time that I get to sorely disappoint you. "Feed a man a fish and he will eat for a day, but teach a man to fish and he will eat for a lifetime." That old axiom pretty well sums up why I don't believe in giving away easy answers. Besides, why take my word for it? Test what you and your kids are reading against a much surer scale; God's Word.

> "You are not only responsible for what you say, but also for what you do not say."
>
> ~Martin Luther

I will say that there are certainly plenty of books out there that Christians have no business reading. This can usually be discovered pre-emptively by reading reviews online; if not, it generally doesn't take more than a few pages to figure out that what you're reading is not God-pleasing material. As Paul writes, "Whatever is true, whatever is noble, whatever is right, whatever is pure, whatever is lovely, whatever is admirable – if anything is excellent of praiseworthy – think about such things" (Phil. 4:8).

The things we think about tend to reflect the things we read about (or watch in movies or play in video games, etc.). The fantasy genre is loaded with rich, noble content that reflects the epic struggle between good and evil that Christians face on a daily basis. Make sure that *this* is the focus of what you are reading, watching, or playing; not the occult powers, foul language, lewd acts, or blood and gore that can sometimes spoil an otherwise good story in any genre. There are plenty of excellent books, movies, and games out there that can teach and inspire Christian warriors without marginalizing or even promoting sinful behavior.

No matter how old you are, God has given you a distinct honor and privilege in the opportunity to serve as a guide to others. With this privilege comes a responsibility to know Scripture and understand how to apply both the Law and the Gospel to our own lives and the situations of others. No one accidentally stumbles upon your journey while you are on the quest. God has placed them in your path for a reason; that you might minister to their needs.

> *"He that takes truth for his guide, and duty for his end, may safely trust to God's providence to lead him aright."*
>
> ~Blaise Pascal

Whether it's your children, students, friends, coworkers, or anyone else around you, there are people with whom you can share your insights, inspiring and teaching them to fight bravely for Jesus' sake. But the first step to being a "wise and helpful guide" is having a thorough knowledge of God's will – which is revealed to us through His Word – and allowing that will to change your heart and mind. We should rely on nothing else, nothing of our own, to guide and direct our own steps and the paths of others. "Do not conform any longer to the pattern of this world, but be transformed by the renewing of your mind. Then you will be able to test and approve what God's will is – His good, pleasing and perfect will" (Romans 12:2).

There you have it. St. Paul says it better than I ever could; God's Word gives us the "mystical insight or transformation of consciousness" we need to be effective warriors and wise guides for others. If we remain firmly planted in the Word and make Scripture our primary reading material, it will never be difficult to discern the good from the bad in the books, movies, and games all around us. And we can use this understanding to help others – especially those over whom God has given us special charge – to make spiritually healthy choices in what they read, watch, and play as well.

> *"How, child, do I know where you're headed? Because I'm there, and I can see you coming."*
>
> *~Robert Brault*

Redeeming the Neutral

There can be a tendency among God's people to look at anything which is not patently Christian as "evil," "secular," or "worldly." While there *are* a good deal of things in this world for which those descriptions are perfectly true and applicable, there are also a great many that could be described by such words as "true," "noble," "right," "pure," "lovely," "admirable," etc. While they may not always mention God or Christ by name, they promote the same values and characteristics that the Church emphasizes. God's Word has "redeemed" many things in our society, even when the authors or creators of those things don't realize it. God's grace is so powerful that it continues to work in our fallen and depraved world through otherwise "secular" sources. Are there "non-Christian" songs out there that teach good lessons or morals? Absolutely, and why would we want to see them silenced?

As Jesus tells his disciples in Mark 9:40, "whoever is not against us is for us." There are many secular songs, books, movies, games, and television shows that – although they don't invoke Jesus' name – are still Godly in content and essence. And just because something isn't explicitly Christian doesn't mean that Christians have to avoid it. Satan is always busy converting "good" things to wicked, sinful purposes; why shouldn't we convert some of the "morally neutral" ones to God's service?

When I was in high school, a group of my friends and I occasionally played the popular role-playing dice game

Dungeons and Dragons (insert shocked gasps of horror here). I know, I know; that game has a reputation for being nefariously evil with its magic and demons and...well, pretty much everything described in this book. As a young Christian man who was trying hard to be a pillar of morality and faithfulness (um, yeah), I *did* feel pretty guilty about my involvement with such a wicked tool of the Devil. Lots of teenagers reveal some dark secret from their past to their parents later in life, and I desperately hope reading this doesn't come as too great a shock to my own folks.

Anyway, the thing I came to realize is that God's presence in my life was much more powerful that any of the dangers that a fantasy role-playing game could ever present. I suppose there are definitely some people out there who were led into rather unsavory pursuits because of their weekend gaming habits, but I would have trouble believing that God was a real big part of their lives to begin with. For my part, I certainly can't say that I was ever a perfect little Christian by any stretch of the imagination, but God's promise held true despite *my* weakness; "My Father, who has given them to me, is greater than all; no one can snatch them out of my Father's hand" (John 10:29).

Despite all of the spiritual hazards and temptations in my teenage years (of which *Dungeons and Dragons* was by no means the greatest), God faithfully preserved me in the faith through the regular hearing of His Word (shout out to my parents here, if they survived the shock of recent revelations).

In fact, as the "Dungeon Master" of my group – that is, the guy who plans the story and encounters for each gaming session – I was able to run campaigns that were overtly "Christian" quite often.

One player in our group was not Christian; in fact, his "other" friends in another state (his parents were divorced) practiced Wicca, which he also became involved in. He once told us, "When I'm with you guys and playing *Dungeons and Dragons*, I start to believe in God again and think about how awesome He is." Now *that* was a cool moment for us – who would have ever thought that *Dungeons and Dragons* could be used to witness for Christ?

> *"I have become all things to all men so that by all possible means I might save some."*
>
> *~1 Corinthians 9:22*

There are many, many other things in this world that have just as great a potential in the clumsy hands of weak, fledgling Christians. *God's* power is at work in our lives, and everything we do should reflect the transformation of mind that we have undergone by means of our faith. "So whether you eat or drink or whatever you do, do it all for the glory of God" (1 Cor. 10:31). The books we read can be understood and interpreted from a Christian standpoint. The movies we watch can be discussed in light of Scriptural truth. The games we play can be played in such a way that they strengthen our faith and glorify our Father in heaven.

We will not abandon this world to the darkness. We will fight for it boldly, even sacrificing when necessary. We will convert whatever is at hand into a weapon that can be used to crush and bludgeon Satan's minions – the fears, the doubts, the temptations, and the misfortunes that assail our friends and neighbors. We will turn the Devil's own trick against him and bend everything we touch into something that glorifies God. After all, if His power can make something good out of a sinful wretch like me, then there is nothing in this world which His love cannot redeem.

> *"And when the fight is fierce, the warfare long, steals on the ear the distant triumph song, and hearts are brave again, and arms are strong."*
>
> ~William W. How: For All the Saints